LOUIS ARMSTRONG

—African-American Biographies—

LOUIS ARMSTRONG

King of Jazz

Series Consultant:
Dr. Russell L. Adams, Chairman
Department of Afro-American Studies, Howard University

Wendie C. Old

Enslow Publishers, Inc.

44 Fadem Road   PO Box 38
Box 699   Aldershot
Springfield, NJ 07081   Hants GU12 6BP
USA   UK

Library of Congress Cataloging-in-Publication Data

Old, Wendie C.
    Louis Armstrong : king of jazz / Wendie C. Old.
        p.   cm. — (African-American biographies)
    Includes bibliographical references (p. 120) and index.
    Summary: Explores the life and career of the renowned trumpeter and
bandleader of the jazz era.
    ISBN 0-89490-997-5
    1. Armstrong, Louis, 1900-1971—Juvenile literature. 2. Jazz
musicians—United States—Biography—Juvenile literature. [1. Armstrong,
Louis, 1900-1971. 2. Musicians. 3. Afro-Americans—Biography. 4. Jazz.]
I. Title. II. Series.
ML3930.A75043   1998
781.65'092—dc21
    [B]   97-35860
                                                                  CIP
                                                                 AC MN
Printed in the United States of America

10 9 8 7 6 5 4 3 2 1

Illustration Credits: Courtesy of the Joseph Merrick Jones Steamboat
Collection, Manuscripts Department, Howard-Tilton Memorial Library,
Tulane University, p. 9; Courtesy of the Louis Armstrong Middle School,
pp. 112, 114; Courtesy of the National Archives, pp. 11, 48, 53, 80, 105,
107; Hogan Jazz Archive, Howard-Tilton Memorial Library, Tulane
University, pp. 18, 62; Louis Armstrong House & Archives at Queens
College/CUNY, pp. 6, 13, 30, 43, 77, 88; *New York World-Telegram & Sun*
Collection, Prints and Photographs Division, Library of Congress, pp.
65, 68, 72, 83, 91, 93, 94, 97, 100; Permission granted from the *Los
Angeles Times*, p. 108; Prints and Photographs Division, Library of Congress,
pp. 33, 38; UPI Photograph, *New York World-Telegram & Sun* Collection,
Prints and Photographs Division, Library of Congress, p. 102.

Cover Illustration: Louis Armstrong House & Archives at Queens
College/CUNY

CONTENTS

Louis Armstrong

1

A HORN IN THE NIGHT

O n a quiet night in 1921, a trombone player named Jack Teagarden wandered with a friend through the French Quarter of New Orleans. Far off in the distance, the lights of a passenger steamboat glided through the mist. The sound of music drifted over the water.

Teagarden describes his meeting Louis Armstrong this way: "The boat was still far off, but in the bow I could see a Negro standing in the wind, holding a trumpet high and filling the night with the hottest, the sweetest, the purest jazz I'd ever heard. . . . I stayed absolutely still, just listening, until the boat dropped anchor. . . ."[1]

When the boat docked, Teagarden ran up the gangplank to meet the unknown horn player with the round, open face. They would become friends, performing together off and on for the rest of their lives.

Armstrong had been playing in jazz bands aboard the steamboats cruising the Mississippi River since 1919. These riverboats brought the New Orleans jazz sound to the rest of the country. Armstrong was part of the beginning. He became the leader among those who spread the music throughout the world.

In the previous century, these riverboats had been important haulers of freight up and down the rivers and the canals connecting them. But with the development of the railroads crisscrossing the country, many riverboat lines went out of business. However, Joe Streckfus was determined that his riverboat line would not go out of business. He simply changed his business—from hauling freight to entertaining people.

He called his boats "excursion boats." In the winter months his boats used New Orleans, Louisiana, as their home port. On weekends the boats would take passengers for a short trip up the river. On these excursions, they offered food and drinks. A band on the upper deck would play music for dancing. This idea was so popular that these excursion riverboats are still in business today.

From May through November, the riverboats took long trips from New Orleans north to St. Paul,

□□□□□□□□□□□□□□□□□□□□□□□□□□□□□□□□□□□□□□

Sunday Excursions
Sept. 18
$1 .oo Trips for 75c Round Trip

"CAPITOL" STEAMER DE LUXE

TWO BIG TRIPS

AFTERNOON
Lv. Memphis - 3:00 P. M.
Rt. 5:30 P. M.

MOONLIGHT
Lv. Memphis - 8:30 P. M.
Rt. 11:30 P. M.

GO "CAPITOLING"

Music - Dancing

GAY PARTY NIGHT

(Over)

Louis Armstrong played in jazz bands aboard steamboats that cruised along the Mississippi River.

Minnesota, more than one thousand miles upriver. The boats stopped at each port along the river.

To attract customers, the bandleader would play cheerful tunes on the shipboard calliope. This instrument looks like an organ and is powered by steam from the boat's engines. Its sound carries for quite a distance. When a good-sized crowd of townspeople had gathered to see what all the noise was about, they would be offered tickets for an evening's trip on the river.

Streckfus hired Fate Marable from the African-American musicians' union in 1910 to organize the bands aboard the riverboats. Marable demanded a high standard of musical ability and had his pick of the best musicians up and down the river.

At first he chose only white musicians. In 1917 Marable decided to hire some of the young African Americans in New Orleans who were creating jazz, the new hot music. That kind of music attracted him, despite the fact that most of these early jazz musicians couldn't read music.

Young Louis Armstrong was one of the hot young horn players Marable hired. Armstrong had the ability to listen to someone play a song just once and then he could pick up his cornet—an instrument similar to a trumpet—and copy the sound. However, Marable expected everyone in the band to be able to play standard dance music as well as the new jazz. Armstrong

The Fate Marable Band entertains passengers on the S.S. *Capitol.* Fate Marable is at the piano. Armstrong, third from right, blows his cornet.

soon discovered that it was necessary to know how to read all those dots and bars on the sheets of music. Several of the band members helped him learn. His marvelous musical ear allowed him to fake it while he picked up this necessary skill.

Unlike his previous musical gigs, this job was full-time. Armstrong was able to quit his part-time jobs and concentrate on playing his instrument. This concentration on musical performance to the exclusion of all else helped him to polish his style.

At first he performed only for the short day excursions based in the port of New Orleans. In 1920 he graduated to the summer-long trips upriver.

That long voyage upriver was Armstrong's first trip away from home. He was fascinated by the constantly changing scenery along the banks of the river. From New Orleans, the boat slipped through the marshy Mississippi delta in Louisiana on into the state of Mississippi. On the riverbanks of western Tennessee and Kentucky, fields of bluegrass waved.

Larger and larger cities faced the river. This part of the United States had not known slavery and had few African-American citizens. For these and many other northern towns, the excursion steamboats were their first exposure to African Americans and the music of New Orleans. When Armstrong described their reaction, he said, "... the ofays [white people] were not used to seeing colored boys making fine music for them to dance by."[2]

Armstrong's ready smile and outgoing nature made him popular with the shipboard audiences. The pleasure he took in performing music was contagious. The more he enjoyed what he was doing, the more the audience enjoyed the show.

His improvised solos on the cornet proved to be as popular in the North as they were in New Orleans.

Louis Armstrong's ready smile and outgoing personality made him a hugely popular entertainer.

Legend has it that Armstrong could start a solo when he was ten miles upriver and still be playing variations of it when the boat reached the dock.[3]

In 1922 Armstrong received an invitation to play with the best jazz band in Chicago, perhaps the best in the world—Joe Oliver's Creole Jazz Band.

Armstrong thought about this offer. If he took the job, he would be nine hundred miles from home. He would have no backup jobs if this one failed. No one there would know his reputation on the river. In addition, he had known many musicians who left New Orleans with high hopes, only to return poor and hungry. Would the same thing happen to him?

On the other hand, Joe Oliver was Armstrong's musical hero and his friend. It was the opportunity of a lifetime. Armstrong decided to grab it. The twenty-two-year-old musician boarded a northbound train on August 8, 1922, and stepped into history.

2

ON THE STREETS
OF NEW ORLEANS

usic has been in my blood from the day I was born," Louis Armstrong often bragged.[1] He celebrated the Fourth of July as his birthday throughout his whole life. His mother told him he was born July 4, 1900. She said she knew it was the Fourth of July because two men were killed in a knife fight that night right outside the house in New Orleans. His family called him the firecracker baby.

Many people could not read or write in those days, and they used the trick of remembering which major holiday was celebrated near their actual birthday. Many babies were born at home at that time, instead of in hospitals. Often there was no official birth certificate registered for home births. None has been found for Louis Armstrong. A recently discovered baptismal record, however, indicates that he was born August 4, 1901.[2]

Louis was surrounded by music while growing up. It floated out of the nearby honky-tonks, cheap gin joints, and saloons. Street musicians wandered by, passing a hat to make a living. German and Italian brass bands played free outdoor concerts. They featured marches, waltzes, polkas, schottisches, and galops.

Like most towns, New Orleans was divided into different areas where people lived and worked. Creoles lived downtown. Most of these people spoke French or Creole. The Creole language is French with a mix of Spanish and African words. That is why this area is often called the French Quarter. The Creole people themselves are a mixture of these three kinds of settlers of the New Orleans area—French, Spanish, and Africans.

West End and Spanish Fort were popular summer resorts. Uptown was where the English-speaking people settled. The city stretched along the Mississippi River. The waterfront area was called Front o' Town.

Little Louie was not born in any of these areas. He was born in his grandmother Josephine Armstrong's two-room house in Back o' Town. This was a poor area of row houses built on what had been a swamp behind the French Quarter. It was such a rough area that it was called the Battlefield. People carrying knives and guns lived next to good churchgoing people. Lots of children played in the unpaved streets. Every city had an area like it where the poorest of the poor lived.

People came to this area to gamble. They visited prostitutes. They bought cheap gin in the honky-tonks and saloons. Here they listened to the African-American music of ragtime and the blues.

Louis remembers Grandmother Armstrong's house as being at 723 James Alley or Jane Alley—a one-block-long street between Gravier and Perdido streets.

His mother, Mary Albert (called Mayann by her family), was sixteen years old when she left the sugarcane-growing area of Boutte, Louisiana, and came to New Orleans. There she met Willie Armstrong, a tall, handsome man who had a steady job as a charcoal burner at a nearby turpentine factory.

Louis Armstrong wrote later that even before he was born, his parents "used to quarrel something awful."[3] Soon after his birth, both of them moved out of Grandmother Armstrong's house to separate living quarters. Little Louie was raised by his grandmother for the first five years of his life. He did not remember meeting his father until he was a teenager.

The women in his family (his grandmother, his great-grandmother, who lived to age ninety, and later his mother) taught him rules of proper conduct. Many

Armstrong's grandmother lived in one of these row houses on Jane Alley in New Orleans. Louis was raised by his grandmother until he was about five years old.

of these rules seemed to be simple common sense to Louis. He claimed: " . . . my good sense and mother-wit and knowing how to treat and respect the feelings of other people, that's all I've needed through life."[4]

When he misbehaved, his grandmother punished him. She would send Louis to get a switch from the big old chinaball tree in her yard. Naturally, he'd come back with the smallest one he could find. This would make her laugh and forget about the switching. However, if she were really mad, she'd whip him for everything he'd done in the past few weeks. Mayann did the same when Louis later lived with her.

Because of this guidance, his values were different from the values of many of the other children in the tough neighborhood in which he was raised. Still, he could act tough when it was necessary in order to survive the constant fights among the children and the grown-ups. His sense of humor also helped in these situations.

His grandmother, an ex-slave, took in washing and ironing to make a living. She made sure Louis attended school, church, and Sunday school. He developed his love for music in church. He threw his whole heart into every song he sang. At that time his voice was a high, clear tenor. Louis Armstrong never lost the churchgoing habit. He attended church throughout his life whenever he could.

His grandmother also introduced Louis to New Orleans–style voodoo. This is a woman-centered religion that blends African, Caribbean, Catholic, and Protestant beliefs. The music of voodoo also influenced his musical development.

His great-grandmother told him tales of life in their African homeland. At the time, the country was known as the Gold Coast. Now it is called Ghana.

When Louis was about five years old, a woman came to take him to his mother. Mayann was sick and there was no one at home to take care of her and his little sister, Beatrice, born in 1903.

When Louis and the woman boarded the streetcar, there were many empty seats up front. Little Louis could not read yet. He did not realize that the seats in the back half of the streetcar had signs saying FOR COLORED PASSENGERS ONLY. He plopped down in a front seat, eager to see where the bus was going.

"Come here, boy," the woman shouted. "Sit where you belong."[5] Louis could not believe she meant it. He made faces at her and stayed put. The woman marched right up to him and jerked him out of the front seat. She ignored his complaints. She dragged him to one of the back seats and plunked him into it. This was his first experience with Jim Crow laws, but not his last.

Jim Crow was the term used for laws that segregated, or kept separate, all people of color from the so-called white people. African Americans were forced to endure this discrimination because of laws enacted in the 1880s and 1890s after the Civil War. The term *Jim Crow* referred to a blackface character (usually a white man with burned cork smeared on his face) in a minstrel show of the 1830s. The character performed a song-and-dance routine called "Jump Jim Crow." This song became associated with segregation.

The Jim Crow laws made it illegal for people of color to use white-designated parts of streetcars, railroad cars, rest rooms, schools, parks, restaurants, and water fountains. These laws also often affected a town's zoning laws, forcing African Americans to accept the poorest housing. However, sometimes the blacks on a streetcar outnumbered the white folk. Then the African Americans took seats as far toward the front as they dared. Louis remembered, "It felt good to sit up there once in a while."[6]

To stay alive, a young African American needed to be brought up to be courteous and to mind his manners. This included not being rude or sassy to adults or white people. The dignified courtesy Louis learned in his early years helped him succeed in the entertainment world as an adult.

Soon after young Louis arrived to help with the baby, Mayann recovered. She went back to work as a maid for a white family who lived on Canal Street, near the City Park Cemetery.

Few people then could afford doctors. A visit to a doctor cost at least fifty cents and might not cure you after all. Mayann's weekly salary was much less than that. Therefore, the family ate their red beans and rice and took home remedies to stay healthy—usually Coal Roller Pills or boiled lemon grass.

When they wanted fruits and vegetables, Louis would go to the big New Orleans farmers markets. There he dug through the piles of damaged and unwanted fruits and vegetables, bringing the best of the lot back to Beatrice and his mother.

His mother lived at Liberty and Perdido. This was a worse neighborhood than his grandmother's. Whereas Grandmother Armstrong lived in a ten-year-old, sturdily built row house, Louis's mother lived in one room of a broken-down shanty.

In spite of that, everyone, from the church folks to the lowest, respected his mother. Louis Armstrong later wrote, "She held up her head at all times. . . . What she didn't have, she did without. She never envied no one, or anything they may have. I guess I inherited that part of life from Mayann."[7]

At least six different men moved in with his mother over the years. Louis called the men stepfathers. When no man was living with her, Louis's mother would sometimes go out on the town for days and days. When she did this, she left Louis and Beatrice with her cousin, Ike Miles. The children called him Uncle Ike. Louis had no idea what his mother did when she was away from her children. Whatever she did, "she kept it out of my sight," he said.[8]

Uncle Ike would take them to live with his own brood of seven children. His wife had died. He worked as a stevedore on the docks of New Orleans, which are called levees, unloading boats to pay for their food and their one-room place.

All the children ran around barefoot. As in many

towns of that time, the streets were just dirt, not paved. Bare feet sometimes picked up a nail, a splinter, or a piece of glass, but most of the children survived. They were young and healthy, and the calluses on their feet were as tough as shoe leather.

At school, Louis was skipped from kindergarten into the second grade. He grew up in this rough area, running with the older kids, learning to shoot dice for pennies and to play blackjack. When he won, he ran to pour the money onto his mother's lap. He loved his grandmother, but he adored his mother and would hear nothing bad about her.

Although the grown-ups called him "Little Louie," his pals had other names for him. Most boys call one another by the most awful names, usually picking on one outstanding characteristic, like hair or ears. With Louis it was his wide, flexible mouth.

At that time, drinking water was kept in a bucket. A long-handled ladle, called a dipper, was used to dip the water from the bucket and pour it into a cup or pan. Many kids drank directly from the dipper. Most people took small neat sips. When Louis was showing off, he could almost swallow the whole bowl of the dipper. Therefore, one of his nicknames became "Dipper." Another nickname was "Gatemouth" or just plain "Gate." Eventually people called him "Satchelmouth," implying that his mouth was big enough to be a suitcase, or a satchel as it was called in those days.

Louis was too young to enter the nearby honky-tonks and dance halls. He could, however, listen to the music that floated out into the street. Sometimes a band would play for half an hour outside a building to attract customers. The children would stand nearby or dance to the music until the band went inside. Louis especially admired cornet and trumpet players like Joe Oliver.

To help bring in money to support his family, he began to sell newspapers after school when he was seven. His boss was an older white boy named Charles. Charles took the place of a big brother to Louis and some of the other newsboys.

When Louis got older, he had a job on the Karnofsky family's junk wagon. The Karnofskys were Russian Jewish immigrants who bought and sold rags, bones, bottles, or whatever else people had to sell. The driver of the junk wagon used a long tin horn to call the people out of their houses. Often he let Louis blow the horn. Louis bragged that "the kids . . . loved the sound of my tin horn."[9]

Eventually, Louis wondered what playing a real horn would be like. He saw a cornet in a pawnshop window for five dollars. That was much more than he earned in a week working on the junk wagon. The Karnofskys lent him the money for the cornet. It was fairly dirty, but it was beautiful in Louis's eyes. It took many weeks for Louis to pay them back. He practiced and practiced and figured out how to play basic notes on the instrument. The little cornet went back into the pawnshop whenever Louis needed money.

When he was about ten, Louis and three other boys discovered they could make money singing. They became street singers. The lead singer and the tenor—Louis—would walk down the street in the Storyville area of town followed by the baritone and the bass. They would sing religious songs and popular songs. They even sang barbershop-quartet numbers like "Sweet Adeline." When someone asked for a special tune, the boys would stop and sing it. Then they would pass a hat around, hoping the listeners would be generous and pour money into it. Often they added to their performance by doing what we now call break dancing. This may have been Louis's first experience at being an entertainer.

Charles, his newspaper boss, warned Louis about singing in such a dangerous area. However, the quartet discovered that they made more money singing for prostitutes and gamblers in the Storyville area than they earned in any other part of town. Therefore, they continued to do it—until one New Year's Eve.

New Orleans celebrates the time between Christmas and New Year's with as much noise as on the Fourth of July. Although it was against the law, many would shoot off guns. This was called "Shooting in the New Year."

One New Year's Eve, when Louis was about twelve or thirteen, he and his quartet were out walking and singing. Louis had brought along a .38 pistol someone had left at Mayann's place. They had just finished singing "My Brazilian Beauty" when another boy shot off a cap gun. Not to be outdone, Louis shot off his real gun—bam! bam! bam! It was bigger, better, and louder than the other boy's. He reloaded it with blanks. A little while later he shot it off again.

For a child, using a gun was as illegal then as it is now. Louis was grabbed from behind by a tall white policeman, Detective Edward Holyland. Louis's friends took off as fast as they could. Louis started crying and pleading with the detective, but it was no use. He was taken to juvenile court and charged with firing a gun in a public place. The next day he was sentenced to the Colored Waifs' Home for Boys.

This event changed his life.

3

His Choice Was Music

n his later years, Louis Armstrong treasured his memories of the Colored Waifs' Home for Boys the way other people remember their college years. The reform school was located on the outskirts of New Orleans, about five miles from Louis's neighborhood. Honeysuckle vines draped themselves all over the grounds. From then on, the smell of honeysuckle on a hot summer day would trigger memories of that time. Honeysuckle became his favorite flower for the rest of his life.

The home was a very clean place. The boys did all the work themselves. Louis learned to scrub floors, wash and iron, cook, make beds, and do other housework.

He also learned to play various sports and got a basic grounding in music. All this knowledge helped him survive the years he later spent on the road as a musician.

At first, though, he was homesick. He wouldn't eat. There were no red beans and rice. There were only white beans with no rice. By the third day he was starving. He ate three bowls and never looked back.

The people who ran the place were called wardens or keepers. The boys were called inmates. Both the keepers and the inmates were African Americans.

Professor Peter Davis taught music and vocational training at the home. At first, Davis seemed to hate Louis. He knew Louis came from a bad neighborhood, and he assumed that anyone from Perdido Street would naturally be worthless.

But Louis couldn't stay away from music. He crept into the corner of the band room and listened every time the band practiced. Belonging to the band was a reward for good behavior. What could Louis do if Professor Davis assumed he would always be bad? Louis adapted to the rules and discipline of the home and behaved himself. After about six months, Professor Davis invited Louis to join the band.

Later Louis wrote, "My whole [musical] success goes back to the time I was arrested. . . . Because then I *had* to quit running around and began to learn something. Most of all I began to learn music."[1]

Professor Davis first gave Louis a tambourine. He whipped it so enthusiastically in rhythm with the band that Professor Davis put him on the drums. Later Louis learned to play the alto horn. When the band's bugler was released from the home, Professor Davis asked Louis if he would like to try that instrument. The other bugler had neglected the instrument. It was all green with tarnish. Louis polished it up first thing.

Later Professor Davis gave him a cornet. Louis was delighted. He had a good ear for the melody and could easily remember musical phrases. Now he received proper musical instruction. Professor Davis was an accomplished brass player and taught Louis the proper way to place his mouth to play. He learned to create a clear, solid tone and to attack each note firmly and accurately.

Louis learned classical pieces of music by European composers such as Liszt, Bach, and Mahler. He also memorized the standard popular pieces played by marching bands: "The Washington Post March" and "The Star-Spangled Banner," for example.

Louis practiced and practiced and became so good that Professor Davis made him leader of the brass band. Although the boys in the home were not allowed to leave the grounds, the band was different. The Waifs' band marched in many of the New Orleans parades. This way Louis was also able to see his family and the gang from Perdido Street.

When he was sent to reform school at the Colored Waifs' Home for Boys, Louis Armstrong began to learn about music. Captain Joseph Jones, the director of the home in 1931, is shown in the upper-right corner of this postcard.

The judge had not set a certain number of years for Louis to serve in the Waifs' Home. Louis had to remain there until either the judge set him free or some important white person vouched for both Louis and his family.

Louis's father had worked his way into positions of more and more responsibility at the turpentine plant. When Louis was fourteen years old, his father had become a supervisor. At this time, very few African Americans achieved such a high position. It was quite unusual for an African American to have the power to hire and fire African Americans working under him. Willie Armstrong persuaded his boss to appeal for Louis's release.

The judge allowed Louis to be released into the custody of his father on June 16, 1914. For a while, Louis lived with his father and stepmother, Gertrude, taking care of their two children—his stepbrothers Henry and Willie.

Since Louis's father and Gertrude both worked, Louis began preparing dinner. The boys loved Louis's red beans and rice. Sometimes they would eat everything so fast that there was none left for Louis. He got into the habit of eating his share before he served the children. When his stepmother discovered she was expecting another child, Louis was sent back to his mother.

Louis Armstrong was finished with school, although he had gone only as far as completing fifth grade, not counting the education at the Waifs' Home. For the next few years, he supported himself with odd jobs. It seemed to him that the people who made the most money in his neighborhood were gamblers and pimps. At first he tried to copy their activities.

From an early age he joined small groups of friends gambling on street corners. He found he had no success with cards. The joy on his open face would reveal every good card he got. He was more successful with dice and other forms of gambling. Every time he won, he gave most of his winnings to his mother and sister. However, music interested Louis more than gambling.

He worked at hauling coal during the day and hung around musicians at night. They began asking him to hold their instruments when they took a break from playing. As they got to know him, they asked him to sit in with them and play. Then he got a steady evening job at a honky-tonk owned by a Frenchman named Ponce.

Most honky-tonks were built with three rooms, front to back. The first was the saloon where drinks were sold. The second was a gambling room. Louis played in the third room, which was for dancing. Honky-tonks did not close until four in the morning during the week. They stayed open all night on Saturday. Each evening, Mayann packed him a lunch so that he need not spend his money on food.

Armstrong would play at the honky-tonk, go home, sleep two hours, then go to work for the C. A. Andrews Coal Company, hauling coal with one of his ex-stepfathers, Gabe. Louis got along with Gabe better than with any of his other stepfathers. No matter how much he begged, however, Mayann wouldn't take Gabe back.

When Ponce's honky-tonk was closed, Louis tried other types of work. He helped unload banana boats. This lasted until a huge rat jumped out of a bunch he

Armstrong worked for a short time unloading bananas, as the men in this picture are doing.

was carrying. Louis dropped that bunch and was not able to eat bananas ever again.

He helped deliver early-morning milk for the Cloverdale Milk Company until he fell off the milk wagon. The milk wagon kept going, and one of the wheels ran over his foot, injuring it. He spent some time as a construction worker. He worked as a building wrecker, a whitewasher, and a dishwasher, and then went back to hauling coal. All the while he found occasional odd jobs in the evening playing his cornet.

Usually he played in honky-tonks as part of a trio—cornet, drum, and piano. Honky-tonks were not looking for good musicians, just ones willing to play most of the night for low pay and tips. The music was not difficult. The prostitutes working in these places preferred the band to play slow blues music that they could dance to.

Because of the prostitution, the gambling room, and the fact that criminals liked to hang out there, honky-tonks were often raided by the police. As a result, Louis was in and out of jail more times than he could remember.

In a letter to one of his biographers, he described his growing fame in New Orleans:

> One morning, on my way to court, the prisoners raked pans on their cell bars and applauded so thunderously, saying "Louis . . . Louis Armstrong," until the guy who was taking me to court said: "Who are you, anyway?" I

said to him, "Oh, just one of the cats." And that's how it has always been.[2]

This cat became a hot cornet player. When musicians say that a fellow player is hot, they do not mean body heat. They also do not mean loud or fast. A hot performer leaves the written music, plays all around it, and then gets back to the melody. As Louis Armstrong explained, it is "when a . . . player . . . 'feels' the music taking hold of him so strong that he can [take the] . . . rhythms and the melody and toss them around as he wants without losing his way."[3]

Many of the musicians performing the new jazz music Louis heard in New Orleans went on to become famous, men such as Buddy Bolden and Jelly Roll Morton. Bunk Johnson had the sweetest tone on the cornet. Sidney Bechet played clarinet and saxophone.

Freddie Keppard would cover the valves of his horn with a handkerchief so that other cornetists could not see his fingering. This didn't protect Armstrong from copying his style. Louis had a perfect musical ear. Once he heard something, he could work out the fingering for himself, and he knew it for life.

The king of the hot cornet players, however, was Joseph Oliver. He played in the top New Orleans band, which was run by the Creole trombonist Edward "Kid" Ory.

One day in 1916, Mutt Carey, the second cornet in Ory's band, needed a break. He let Armstrong sit in his place. Louis played each chorus a little bit differently, yet it was still the blues. At the end of that set, Carey kidded him, saying, "Louis, you keep playing that horn and some day you'll be a great man."[4]

Joe Oliver was also impressed. He took Armstrong under his wing. Armstrong ran errands for Oliver and his wife, Stella. They became Louis's second family. For the rest of his life, Armstrong called Oliver "Papa Joe." Armstrong later said, "I can never stop loving Joe Oliver."[5]

Oliver repaid him by giving him cornet lessons. They played duets together. He told Louis to keep two things in mind. First, he should strive to play a clear, round tone. Second, he should always play the lead—which is also called the basic melody.

Seeing that Armstrong kept borrowing cornets for performances, Oliver gave him his old, beat-up York cornet. Even so, this cornet also went in and out of pawnshops, depending on which Armstrong needed more at the moment—cash or a horn to play.

All the African-American horn players in New Orleans blew cornets. The large white orchestras had trumpet players. Armstrong says that his group of musicians thought a person had to have a music conservatory degree or be a high muckety-muck to be allowed to play the trumpet. As a result, he didn't even try playing the trumpet until years later.

New Orleans needed little excuse to hold a parade,

and Armstrong played in marching bands in most of them. The bands he belonged to were also hired to play for funerals. There was a strict format to New Orleans funerals. From the church to the cemetery the band would play slow, sad hymns. The drum would have a piece of cloth between the bottom head and the snares to create a dull, muffled thud. Then, after the casket had been put in the vault, the drummer removed the cloth. The band led the crowd back with raucous, loud tunes such as "Didn't He Ramble," celebrating life and the afterlife.

The biggest New Orleans parades were during Mardi Gras, which is celebrated right before the Christian period of Lent. Each parade is organized by a different social club. The first African-American organization to be allowed to hold a Mardi Gras parade was the Zulu Aid Pleasure and Social Club. This club was organized in 1909. Its name, taken from a famous tribal group in Africa, reflected the members' pride in their African heritage.

In a Mardi Gras parade, members dress up with wild makeup, pretending to be famous persons. The brass band plays good jumping music. The King of the Zulus rides on a float. He and six others toss trinkets and coconuts to the wildly cheering crowd. It is no wonder that every boy in the neighborhood wanted to be King of the Zulus when he grew up.

In 1917 America entered World War I. Several

Armstrong participated in funeral processions that marched to cemeteries like this one. Since the city of New Orleans is below sea level, it is not possible to bury the dead underground. Instead they are buried in above-ground vaults.

Navy men stationed in New Orleans visited prostitutes in the Storyville area and were murdered. There was an immediate government reaction. On November 14, 1917, the U.S. Navy closed Storyville down. Many of the musicians who had made their living entertaining in or near that area drifted away. Some went north to fame and fortune. Others found no fame or money. These men came crawling back to their families.

A law was passed ordering men to work or fight in the armed forces. Armstrong felt himself lucky to have the job hauling coal. He says he quit that job the minute he heard the war was over on November 11, 1918.

Earlier in 1918, Armstrong fell in love and married a Creole woman named Daisy Parker. He described their relationship as four years of torture and bliss. Daisy could not read or write. All she wanted to do was have a good time or fight.

One time she saw Armstrong talking to an old girl-friend. She whipped out her straight razor and ran for him. He was faster, but he lost his prized Stetson hat that he had saved so many months to buy. She slashed it to ribbons. Another time their argument grew, ending with their throwing bricks at each other.

They lived in a two-room second-floor apartment. Like most houses in New Orleans, it had a balcony—a place where they could sit and catch the evening breeze. However, their balcony was partially broken, slanting down toward the alley below.

When Armstrong's cousin Flora needed someone to look after her son, Clarence, Armstrong volunteered. One day little Clarence disappeared from the apartment. They found him lying in the alley below. He had slipped off the balcony and hit his head. The injury caused Clarence to become brain-damaged. Later, when Flora died, Armstrong adopted Clarence. He cared for Clarence for the rest of his life.

In the summer of 1918, Papa Joe Oliver left New Orleans for the greener musical pastures of Chicago. A huge crowd, including Armstrong, gathered to see him off. Just before the train took off, Oliver suggested Armstrong take his place in Kid Ory's Band.

By this time Armstrong had learned every piece Ory's band played. He fit right in. It was with this band that Armstrong worked up a little "jive" routine, as he called it. He said he would do "a little tap dancing and a little fooling around between the numbers to get laughs."[6]

He also wrote and sold some songs. "I Wish I Could Shimmy Like My Sister Kate" became a big hit. Armstrong sold all rights to it for $50. He didn't own the rights to another New Orleans jazz standard that he had written. Kid Ory named the tune "Muskrat Ramble." When asked about this in the 1960s,

Armstrong said, "Ory named it, he gets the royalties. I don't talk about it."[7]

It was customary for New Orleans bands to be pulled through the streets on a wagon to advertise the dance hall featuring their band that night. Whenever one bandwagon met another at a cross street, they would have a "cutting" contest to see which band was better than the other. Musicians call their instruments axes that cut (play) music.

One afternoon in 1919 a man stood listening to a cutting contest on a street corner. This man had the power to change Louis Armstrong's life. Fate Marable worked for the Streckfus riverboat company, organizing bands to entertain the passengers. He had been looking to hire some of the young African Americans in New Orleans who were creating the new hot music. He wanted only the best musicians—and he made no mistake when he chose Louis Armstrong.

He hired Armstrong to perform on the day excursions that left from the port of New Orleans. In 1920, Armstrong began playing on the steamer *Dixie Belle*, which took summer-long trips upriver. During the long riverboat voyages for the next few years, Armstrong had time to think about his unhappy marriage to Daisy Parker, and about life in general. He also learned to read music.

There was no other black orchestra going up and down the Mississippi. When they reached the middle of the country they had to put up with a lot of nasty remarks from the whites. But the band members knew what was expected of them. They didn't mingle with the white passengers. They also knew that the minute they began to play, those passengers sat up and took notice and by the end of the night were enjoying themselves.

Armstrong learned a lot from observing others. He watched one of the musicians nearly starve himself trying to save money. The musician invested all his savings in cotton farming. Boll weevils ate up the crop. Instead of doubling his money, the musician lost all his savings. Armstrong promised himself that this would never happen to him. He decided, "I'll never be rich, but I'll be a fat man."[8]

In 1921, Fletcher Henderson, who had a well-paying job at the Roseland Ballroom on Broadway in New York City, asked Armstrong to come join his band, but Armstrong refused to leave his hometown and his family and friends.

Armstrong got another musical job, with the Tuxedo Brass Band, the best marching band in New Orleans. They marched with their music written on stiff cards perched on their horns. It was a good thing Armstrong had learned to read music on the riverboat.

Papa Joe Oliver kept sending letters from Chicago. Every letter urged Armstrong to come up north. Finally, in 1922, Armstrong decided to take the plunge.

Before he left for Chicago, Armstrong posed for a portrait with his mother, Mayann, and his sister, Beatrice.

▣▣▣▣▣▣▣▣▣▣▣▣▣▣▣▣▣▣▣▣▣▣▣▣▣▣▣▣▣▣▣▣▣▣▣

He had a family photograph taken of himself, his mother, and his sister.

Then the five-foot-six-inch, plump Little Louie Armstrong boarded the train for Chicago. He took along his typewriter, his record collection, his cornet, a few clothes, and a fish sandwich to eat on the trip. African Americans were not allowed to eat in the train dining car.

It would be years before he came back.

4

JAZZ IN THE
ROARING
TWENTIES

o one met him in Chicago. Armstrong hung around the railroad station for half an hour before he got the courage to ask someone for help. It turned out that Joe Oliver had been waiting for him but had to leave when Armstrong did not show up at the scheduled time. It was Armstrong's own fault. He had stayed longer in New Orleans to play in a funeral to earn some spending money for the trip to Chicago. This forced him to take a later train than he had planned.

When Armstrong finally reached the Lincoln Gardens on the South Side of Chicago, where King Oliver's Creole Jazz Band was performing, he met the band. Armstrong had long known that Joe Oliver was the best. However, this was the first time Armstrong heard Oliver called "King Oliver."

After the show, Oliver took him home, where Stella stuffed them both with New Orleans red beans and rice. Then Oliver took Armstrong to a boardinghouse on South Wabash Avenue run by a Creole woman named Filo.

Here Armstrong discovered that each room had a private bath. It was the first time that Armstrong had ever experienced modern indoor plumbing. All his life back home in the Back o' Town of New Orleans he had used outhouses and a small tin tub for washing.

After a week of rehearsal, Armstrong opened with King Oliver's band as second cornetist. Much later, when Armstrong talked about that opening night, the main thing he remembered was the butterflies in his stomach. He remarked that you never escaped the butterflies, no matter how long you've been in this business. Opening night is always the same—more butterflies.[1]

The band was a huge success, playing a half hour overtime at each show. They wowed listeners with what seemed to be improvised duets by Oliver and Armstrong. Actually, the duet breaks depended upon Armstrong's marvelous ear. A few minutes before the duet was to begin, Oliver would play the theme he was going to use. Then the two of them stood up and took off musically. Armstrong supported that theme with his own just-created harmonizing countertheme.

Lillian "Lil" Harden, a graduate of Fisk University in Memphis, Tennessee, then an African-American women's college, rejoined the band a few months later on piano. She had trained in a musical conservatory as a classical pianist but preferred playing jazz. Her first impression of Armstrong was that he wore clothes too small for him, with an atrocious tie dangling over a huge stomach. The worst part of the whole picture was Armstrong's bangs. Wearing bangs was the latest style among musicians in New Orleans, but Armstrong's bangs did not lie flat on his forehead. They jutted out in front of his face like the bill of a cap.

Armstrong weighed 226 pounds. Lil could not figure out why all the musicians called him Little Louie. When she asked, they told her it was only natural, since Armstrong had been hanging around them since he was a little ol' thing.

Mayann came up to Chicago a few months later to check on her son. She had heard that he was sick and not eating, but Armstrong assured her he was doing fine. In fact, he rented an apartment for her and bought her new clothes. She soon missed New Orleans, however, and decided to return home.

Oliver's band went on tour in 1923 through Illinois, Ohio, and Indiana. Sometime between March 31 and April 6, they stopped in Richmond, Indiana, to

Playing with the King Oliver Band, Louis Armstrong (third from right) often improvised duets with King Oliver (seated). At the right is Lil Harden.

make their first recordings at the Starr Piano Company. King Oliver, Bessie Smith, and Jelly Roll Morton all made their first recordings that year. One of the songs the Oliver band recorded, "Chimes Blues," featured the first recording of an Armstrong solo.

The acoustic recording equipment could not handle drums. A drum roll would make the recording needle jump right off the track. There was no microphone. A large horn, like a megaphone, directed the music into the recording equipment.

To top it all, if Oliver and Armstrong stood together for their duets, as they did on the bandstand, Armstrong's volume would drown out all the other instruments. The musicians experimented. Finally they discovered that the perfect musical balance happened when Armstrong played from the back corner of the room, more than fifteen feet away. Even there his high-register notes were often too strong for the recording equipment.

This, more than anything else, convinced Lil Hardin that Armstrong was not only the better cornetist but the best musician she had seen for a long time. Joe Oliver confessed to Lil that "as long as I keep him playing second to me he won't get ahead of me. I'll still be the king."[2] No one else had Oliver's fire and endurance, but now he was thirty-eight years old and he had trained his own successor.

Armstrong was young—in his early twenties. He was a shy, serious man who was eager to please. He had the deep chest and strong lips that could blow hard on any brass horn. Looking back, Armstrong remembered: "In later years they called me 'Iron Lips' Armstrong or 'Brass Lips' because I could blow more high C notes in succession than any swing trumpeter in the world. . . . I like to get way up there and hold on to that clear high note."[3]

Later that year, Armstrong divorced his wife, Daisy. Lil Hardin was his new love. It had taken him a little while to realize that a college-educated woman could be seriously interested in him, a fifth-grade dropout. He married Lil Hardin on February 5, 1924.

Lil convinced Armstrong that there was room for only one lead cornet in Oliver's band—and that one was Oliver. She encouraged him to look for other outlets for his talent, even though she would remain in Chicago. An opportunity came when Fletcher Henderson again invited him to come to New York City.

Henderson's band was performing at the famous Roseland Dance Hall at Broadway and Fifty-first Street. It had been the first African-American dance band to perform there. His band was not a hot jazz band. However, the local African-American press described it as the "greatest, not at all like the average Negro orchestra, but in a class with the good white orchestras."[4]

In May 1924, Armstrong took his place with the band as second or third cornetist. The audience was mostly white people who came to dance the Charleston, the Black Bottom, and the other new dances.

Armstrong also played after-hours dates in Harlem. He recorded with more than fifty popular blues and jazz artists, including the singer Bessie

Smith and soprano saxophonist Sidney Bechet, on records intended for the African-American audience. These records were called "race" records. He was popular in Harlem because of his records. However, to the lower part of Manhattan, where whites lived, he was just another musician in Henderson's band.

Many musicians in Henderson's band who went on to become major figures of the Swing Era, such as Coleman Hawkins, have told how their view of performing jazz was transformed by their exposure to Louis Armstrong's style. Armstrong, however, did not think much of the majority of his fellow band members.

He became tired of Henderson's band members' coming to the bandstand so drunk they couldn't even keep time. He told an interviewer, "When them cats commenced getting careless with their music, fooling around all night, I was dragged, man."[5]

In November 1925, after a year in New York City, Armstrong returned to Lil in Chicago. He had learned many new showmanship tricks. He had improved his music reading and interpreting skills.

Lil was now performing at Bill Bottoms's Dreamland. She created a featured spot for Armstrong there at $75 per week. (He had been getting $55 in New York City.) At this time, the average African-American laborer was getting $10 per week.

To celebrate their reunion, Louis and Lil purchased

a house on East Forty-fourth Street. During this time, the South Side of Chicago was called Bronzeville, or the Black Belt, because so many southern blacks moved there. The Armstrongs also bought a car and some land at Lake Idlewild in Michigan. Clarence moved in with them, as did Lil's mother.

For the next few years, Lil guided Armstrong's musical career. Beginning on November 12, 1925, Armstrong recorded several jazz records with four other musicians. Lil played the piano, supported by Kid Ory on trombone, Johnny Dodds on clarinet, and Johnny St. Cyr on banjo. They called themselves the Hot Five. This group met only for recording. They never performed for an audience.

Okeh (a race label) promoted the records by giving away pictures of Louis Armstrong with every record. Those records flew out of the stores.

In December 1925, Armstrong joined the Erskin Tate Orchestra. This group performed background music for silent movies at the Vendome Theater. Before the movie they played an overture. During breaks in the film they sometimes did solo work onstage.

The brass section was led by Jimmy Tate, who played trumpet. He preferred to have another trumpet player rather than a cornet player in his section. As a result, he suggested that Armstrong switch instruments. From that time on, Armstrong played the trumpet.

Louis Armstrong's Hot Five made a number of popular jazz records. Louis Armstrong is in the center, with Lil Armstrong at the right.

Along with the gig at the theater, Armstrong starred at various nightclubs and cabarets. In 1926, he joined the Carroll Dickerson Band at the Sunset Cafe, a popular South Side nightclub managed by Joe Glaser. Here he saw his name go up in lights for the first time. The lights advertised the headline attraction as "Louis Armstrong, World's Greatest Trumpet Player." He wrote in his autobiography *Swing That*

Music, "I will never forget the kick I got when I first saw that big bright sign."[6]

Louis Armstrong had arrived. He was now the King of Jazz.

White musicians heard about this amazing African-American trumpet player. They packed the Sunset, hoping to learn his tricks. His influence on the rest of the jazz world was recognized by one critic, who wrote, "Louis' phrasing and style were the admitted inspiration for almost every other prominent jazz trumpet player and vocalist. His spontaneous inventions laid the foundation."[7]

Also in 1926, he finally used his now deep, gravely voice to sing on some of his recordings. One friend, the singer and actor Rudy Vallee, described Armstrong's voice as "that utterly mad, hoarse, . . . mumble-jumble that is Louis' 'singing.' . . . beautifully timed and executed . . . [with] a subtle musical understanding [controlled by a] keen mind. . . . "[8]

In the early years of recording, the artist had to play and record the whole piece straight through—no stopping for retakes. It was at this time that Armstrong wrote and recorded the hit song "Heebie Jeebies." He claimed that during the recording of this song, he dropped the sheet music and had to improvise something. As he gathered up the music, he filled in with nonsense syllables instead of the words. This is known as scat singing. Some musicians credit Armstrong with inventing scat.

The singer Bing Crosby listened to Louis Armstrong records when he was young. He made scat his own trademark when he became a famous crooner. Jazz singers use it even today. Some critics in the 1920s described scat as the avant-garde poetry of sound.

Louis Armstrong's Hot Five became his Hot Seven in 1927 with the addition of Baby Dodds on drums and a tuba player. By this time the recording equipment had improved. Now electric microphones carried the sound directly into the machines that recorded the music.

Armstrong stood out from the group with his strong solos on these recordings. They were the basis for his fame among white Americans. He was already popular with African Americans, who attended his concerts in Chicago and on tour. They also read about his lifestyle and his views in the African-American newspapers. In fact, he had become a cultural hero among African Americans.

Louis Armstrong's association with Chicago helped make it one of the midwestern urban centers for African-American culture. Chicago was a national railroad hub. It was the home of one of the largest Hearst newspapers. As the entertainment center of the Midwest, it was a good place to launch a national career.

Chicago was also home to many crime bosses during the Prohibition years, when it was against the law to serve liquor. Like Duke Ellington and many other African-American entertainers, Armstrong knew and worked for gangsters. For Armstrong as well as for the Duke, the music alone mattered, not the person who owned the establishment.

At one point Armstrong was given control of the band he played with. That was when he decided he was not cut out to be a band manager. From then on he let others take care of the nitty-gritty money and personnel aspects of a band. This allowed him to be free just to perform music.

In 1927, Mayann Armstrong made her last visit to Chicago. She died in her son's home on Forty-fourth Street. Armstrong could afford to give her a large, expensive funeral. He later confessed, "Her funeral in Chicago is probably the only time I ever cried."[9]

Many Americans discovered Armstrong's skill with the trumpet from listening to the radio broadcasts from Chicago's Savoy Ballroom. They were heard throughout the Midwest and the northeastern United States, and even in parts of Canada in 1928.

Armstrong's Savoy Ballroom Five recorded a jazz landmark called "West End Blues." It showed some influences of opera in its dazzling introductory cadenza. He was then earning a top pay of $200 a week.

Armstrong knew how to hold an audience's

attention. African-American entertainers at that time were expected to act jolly and sometimes downright silly onstage. Armstrong went along with this. He worked hard within the narrow limits put on African-American performers to create an image popular with whites and African Americans alike. With his friendly, outgoing stage personality, he created gags and jokes. His eternally optimistic outlook also helped. His act delighted audiences out for a good time.

Still, for Armstrong, the music always came first. Although he often made funny faces, joked, grinned from ear to ear, rolled his eyes, and danced onstage, he also would stand motionless for a moment while he improvised on a melody. At times he would draw out an improvisation for twenty minutes. The audience hung on every note.

When the Savoy could no longer pay the band in 1929 (because of a major crackdown on the sale of alcohol), Armstrong and the Carroll Dickerson Band packed up and headed to New York City. Armstrong drove his own 1928 Hupmobile. He had bought it with the royalties from a book of trumpet exercises he had published.

They took the long way, stopping to see tourist sights like Niagara Falls. Armstrong and his fellow musicians were fond of the new box cameras. Some of them even owned amateur movie cameras. As a result, from this time on, there is a ongoing record of informal snapshots of Armstrong's life.

Only two of the cars survived the trip. When the Hupmobile reached Times Square in the heart of New York City, the radiator cap blew off. Immediately, a police officer searched the car full of African Americans for firearms.

The band's first engagement was to replace the Duke Ellington Orchestra at the Audubon Theater. Their next stop would be Broadway.

5

BIG BANDS

rmstrong's manager, Tommy Rockwell, got him a job performing at Connie's Inn in Harlem. The show at this top nightspot rivaled Duke Ellington's at the famous Cotton Club. The show featured singers, dancers, and comedy and specialty acts.

The show was so good that it moved to the Hudson Theater for the 1929–1930 Broadway season. It became one of several African-American musicals on Broadway that featured the new popular music and dance. The show was called *Hot Chocolates*, referring to the many beautiful African-American chorus girls. The music was by Fats Waller and the lyrics were by Andy Razaf and Harry Brooks.

Calling a Broadway show *Hot Chocolates* was considered a complimentary name at that time, with no loss of dignity. Similarly, the famous boxer Joe Louis was known as "The Brown Bomber."

The show got rave reviews. Armstrong began by playing in the orchestra pit, out of sight of the audience. He had a solo song called "Ain't Misbehavin'." When it was recorded and became a hit, he was promoted from the pit to the stage. There he, his friend Waller, and Edith Wilson performed a skit called "One Thousand Pounds of Rhythm." Their joy in performing spilled over the stage and infected the audience.

After each show, Armstrong taxied uptown to head the band at Connie's. For a few weeks he was also featured in a spot in the late show at the Lafayette Theater next door. He jokingly claimed that "[I] had to get my sleep coming through the park in a cab."[1]

Performing in so many places at once trained Armstrong to entertain for the widest mass audience. He performed with many other professional entertainers, including the tap dancer and actor Bill "Bojangles" Robinson. Their example taught him that "the main thing is live for that audience."[2] Louis Armstrong, musician, became Louis Armstrong the entertainer.

His offstage personality was as fascinating to his friends and fans as his onstage one. Musician Rex

Stewart's description of Armstrong in 1929 could easily be that of a modern pop star:

> What he carried with him was the aroma of [spicy] red beans and rice, with more than a hint of voodoo and "gris-gris." He conveyed this to the world by the insouciant challenge of his loping walk, the cap on his head tilted at an angle, which back home meant: "Look out! I'm a bad cat—don't mess with me!"[3]

During the 1930s, Armstrong toured the country many times. In the spring of 1930 he went on a tour of the Northeast as Luis Russell's featured trumpeter. The big-band sound had become popular. From this time on he often was the featured soloist for large bands.

In July, he arrived in Hollywood, California, to perform at Frank Sebastian's Cotton Club in Culver City. Trumpet player Buck Clayton remembered the effect he had when he arrived. Armstrong brought the high style of the Chicago entertainment world to Hollywood and the Los Angeles area with his shiny, processed hair and fashionable clothing. With his suit he wore an ascot tie with an extra large knot. Soon all the hip cats were wearing big knots in their ties and calling them Louis Armstrong knots.[4]

Armstrong stayed in Hollywood for about a year, making records and broadcasting his show nightly. He also began the first of his many appearances in film. He had arrived in Hollywood at just the right moment. Movies were switching from silent films to talkies. Directors were searching for interesting voices.

Louis Armstrong autographed this publicity photograph and sent it to his cousin James.

Armstrong's voice and vibrant personality made him popular in film. His voice was described as gravely, husky, scatty (because he liked to sing scat), optimistic, energetic, and warm and friendly.[5]

During the 1930s, African-American actors usually played comic servants or faithful companions. This presented a view of African Americans that was not threatening to the white world. When Armstrong acted in a film, scenes were written to emphasize his music, both singing and trumpet, in addition to his gift for gab and comedy. He played mostly popular songs and show tunes. His dim-witted dialogue is best forgotten. He played a grinning, easygoing, ever-cheerful, help-ful friend who was always at the hero's beck and call.

In 1931, Armstrong returned to Chicago. However, his relations with Lil were strained. Their different backgrounds led them to expect different things from marriage, and neither of them was happy. Armstrong began seeing Alpha Smith, an adoring young fan.

In addition to the stress in his personal life, New York City and Chicago gangsters were fighting over Armstrong as a professional performer. Al Capone wanted him to stay in Chicago and perform at the Showboat. Gangster boss Dutch Schultz, part owner of Connie's Inn, wanted him back in New York City.

Armstrong quickly escaped this uncomfortable sit-uation by taking his band on tour around the country—away from both New York and Chicago. The group included his new manager, Johnny Collins, and a white bus driver. It was necessary to have both a white bus driver and a white manager in those days. Otherwise, a busload of African Americans could be hassled by law enforcement officers and white citizens alike. They could be accused of being vagrants and bums and then thrown into jail.

Touring the American South was often uncomfortable and sometimes dangerous for African-American musicians in the first half of the twentieth century. When they arrived in a town, they were not allowed to check into the local white hotel. They had to find someplace to stay in the black area of town. Even if they could find a restaurant to let them in, they might not be served. Some places did not even have a bathroom they could use. If there was only one bathroom, it always was for "whites only."

On the other hand, there was quite a turnout in New Orleans for the megastar! Armstrong was met at the train station by the Zulu Aid Pleasure and Social Club's band along with other brass bands, and a huge crowd of both white and black Americans. They paraded him through the city. One company named a cigar after him—the "Louis Armstrong special." A baseball team changed its name to Armstrong's Secret Nine. He agreed to sponsor them and supply their uniforms.

The band was engaged for several months of concerts at the Suburban Gardens. However, when it

Louis Armstrong and his big-band orchestra.

came time for the first concert to begin, Armstrong's friends and neighbors could not attend. Five thousand white people sat in the hall. Ten thousand African Americans had to listen sitting on the levee outside, hoping to hear the music through the open windows.

The concerts were broadcast on radio. That first night, the white announcer began his opening speech, then stopped. There was no way he was going to introduce an African American from the Back o' Town of New Orleans on the radio. He walked off. For a moment there was panic backstage and in the radio control booth. Then Armstrong told his band to play a chord and hold it. He walked out onstage. The ovation was overwhelming. As soon as Armstrong could quiet the crowd, he thanked the audience and began the show.

The announcer was fired on the spot. For the rest of the three-month gig, Armstrong did all the announcing. He attempted to do a special concert for African Americans right before he left town. However, when he arrived for the concert, he discovered the crowd had been told by the police to go home.

America was now deep into the Great Depression. The stock market crash in 1929 had destroyed the finances of millions of people. Many banks were permanently closed. Thousands of businesses had failed. Jobs were scarce. The government had to step in, providing food and jobs to help people survive until times got better.

During one of the coldest weeks of this tour, the Armstrong band performed at the Royal Theater, located in a poor area of Baltimore, Maryland. Armstrong learned that there were people in the neighborhood with no money to buy coal to heat their homes. He went to a coal yard and ordered a ton of coal. When the coal was delivered to the lobby of the Royal Theater, the people in the neighborhood who needed it most were invited to come help themselves, black and white alike. Many of them came backstage after the show to thank him.

Louis Armstrong was so popular that both black and white Americans listened to his radio programs and bought his records. His 1931 hits included humorous songs like "I'll Be Glad When You're Dead, You Rascal, You" and jazz favorites such as Hoagy Carmichael's "Georgia on My Mind" and "Lazy River."

He also recorded "When It's Sleepy Time Down South." This song became his theme song, despite its use of the words *mammies* and *darkey*. Armstrong defended it by saying that he hadn't written the song, he only performed it—as written.[6] (Later he either "scatted" over the objectionable phrases or changed them.) He often did the best he could with silly or offensive lyrics. In concert he sometimes "forgot" the words or changed them to scat.

Armstrong recorded with several singers. The frills and obligatos of his trumpet enhanced their singing. Armstrong thought blues singer Bessie Smith was the greatest of all the singers he accompanied. He declared, "Everything I did with her, I *like*."[7]

In 1932, Louis and Lil formally separated. Their divorce wouldn't be final for several years. One of the many things that had to be settled was the rights to their compositions. Many of their recordings together gave credit to L. Armstrong as composer and arranger.

Armstrong participated in a radio show called *This Is Jazz*. Warren "Baby" Dodds plays the drums, George "Pops" Foster slaps the bass fiddle, and Armstrong leads with the trumpet. Rudi Blesh (far right) directed the show.

Which L. Armstrong was it—Lil or Louis? A court would have to decide.

It was during his first trip to England in 1932 that Armstrong claims his nickname was changed from Satchelmouth to Satchmo. The editor of the English jazz magazine M*elody Maker*, P. Mathison Brooks, called him that when he greeted Armstrong at the boat on July 14. Other sources say that "Satchmo" is just the phonetic spelling of the soft, southern way Armstrong and his African-American friends pronounced "Satchelmouth." In any case, he has been known as Satchmo ever since, even on his gravestone.

That first London trip was not well planned. Johnny Collins was a poor manager. He also drank too much. When they arrived in England, the group discovered the arrangements Collins claimed to have made had not been taken care of. No room reservations had been made ahead of time. They soon discovered that late at night, it was just as difficult for black musicians to find a place to stay in England as it was in the United States. England was segregated, too.

Armstrong came without a backup band. His manager imported black musicians from France for the London concerts. A group of ten white musicians backed Armstrong during the rest of his four months of concerts in England.

Armstrong's "You Rascal, You" was a big hit in Great Britain. He broke the attendance record for a band at London's Palladium Theatre. However, not everyone who came enjoyed hearing him hit high note after high note with little melody in between. There were mass walkouts of unhappy ticket holders.

On the other hand, most of the dedicated English jazz fans were delighted. Jazz expert and biographer Max Jones described Armstrong at a concert as

> a smallish but power-packed figure prowling the stage restlessly, menacingly almost, and growling and gesticulating when he was not playing, singing or talking into the microphone. He addressed his trumpet as though it had life of its own (Speak to 'em, Satchmouth), and controlled the band with faintly alien instructions like "Way down, way down," "Keep muggin' . . . lightly, lightly and politely," and "Swing, swing, swing, you cats."[8]

By this time his manager knew to keep twenty to forty fresh handkerchiefs backstage. Armstrong used them not only to keep the sweat out of his eyes and off the trumpet but also to give signals to the band. It was also a great piece of stage action. That flash of white kept the audience's eyes always on him.

He returned to the United States in November, just after Franklin D. Roosevelt was elected president. Although Armstrong needed to rest his lip, Collins continued to overbook him. He appeared in Connie's *Hot Chocolates of 1932* for a few weeks. He quit the show after his lip finally split as he played the song "Them There Eyes."

Armstrong treated his injury with home remedies—from a useful lip balm to others more painful and more dangerous. Friends said the sore was so large and raw it looked as if he had a strawberry on his lip. After a short rest to let his lip begin to heal, Collins booked him on tours throughout the United States and then back to Europe in August. This time he would stay for eighteen months.

Armstrong could no longer work with Collins, who was drinking too much and keeping all of Armstrong's income. He was not paying Armstrong's bills or sending money to Lil. Armstrong fired his manager and used English and European promoters to arrange bookings in Belgium, Sweden, Denmark, France, Switzerland, and Italy. Ten thousand screaming fans greeted him in Denmark.

From April through October 1934, Armstrong took the longest vacation of his life. He rested his sore lip in sunny Paris, France, where there was no prejudice against black people. He returned to the United States in January 1935.

He went to his old friend Joe Glaser, who used to manage the Sunset Cafe in Chicago, for advice about getting a new manager. They both decided Glaser would be the perfect man, and he was. Until his death, Glaser remained Armstrong's manager. He was unusual in that he was the only white music manager who would travel in the same bus with his African-American client.

Louis Armstrong's improvised solos were legendary.

An interview in *Down Beat* magazine in June 1935 quoted the cheerful Armstrong as saying, "My chops is fine, now . . . and I'm dying to swing out again. They gave me a new trumpet over in Europe, and I've got a smaller mouthpiece than I had on my old horn. . . . I'm all rested up and dying to get going again."[9]

Glaser encouraged Armstrong to emphasize himself as an entertainer, singer, and musician. This brought in more money than a simple musician could earn. Glaser also urged Armstrong to spread his friendly smile far and wide. In fact, eventually all the advertisement needed to announce that Satchmo was coming was a drawing of Armstrong's lips and teeth smiling on a billboard.

Traveling all that time with a typewriter paid off in 1936. Armstrong's first book, *Swing That Music*, was published. Although it was heavily edited and even rewritten in parts by editor Horace Gerlack, it still stands as the very first autobiography of any jazz musician.

Then, in 1937, Armstrong broke another barrier. Without any fanfare, he substituted for his friend Rudy Vallee on the *Fleischmann's Yeast Hour*, a popular radio show. He became the first African American to host a national radio program. This event opened the doors for African-American performers in theaters and clubs around the country.

Joe Oliver did not have many years of performing remaining after Armstrong left him. He developed gum problems, losing his teeth. Without teeth to brace the mouthpiece of his cornet, he was unable to play. For several years before Oliver died on April 10, 1938, Armstrong sent him money to help him out.

Armstrong recorded the anthem of traditional jazz, "When the Saints Go Marching In," in 1938. It became a hit record and has remained an old standby.

During the 1930s Armstrong also returned several times to Hollywood to make films. He was one of the few African Americans who regularly appeared in movies. In the film *Going Places* (1938), he croons the tune "Jeepers Creepers" to a horse with that name. The premise was that the wild and unruly horse would become gentle and controlled only when Armstrong sang to it. This part earned him an Academy Award nomination.

Armstrong had been waiting for his divorce from Lil to become final before he married wife number three, Alpha Smith. Unlike Lil, she was not a musician and therefore could not participate in Armstrong's musical life. They married in October 1938.

Armstrong starred with many big bands through-out the 1930s and 1940s. Yet he never had the desire to lead his own band. He preferred to let others do the worrying about money and attendance. He explained, "I never cared to be a band leader; there was too much quarreling over petty money matters. I just wanted to blow my horn peacefully."[10]

6

KING OF JAZZ

ecause Nazi Germany had condemned jazz, it became the symbol of freedom and liberation for America and the Allies during World War II. The American soldiers introduced jazz and swing music around the world, wherever they were stationed.

During the war, many performers were invited to go overseas to entertain the soldiers. Armstrong appeared at many United States military bases. In between tours, he played his music on Armed Forces Radio. He also made a series of musical recordings for the United States military.

On the home front, Armstrong continued to

perform popular tunes, easily becoming a part of the swing movement in music. A singer as well as a musician, he had become friends with many popular swing crooners such as Rudy Vallee and Bing Crosby.

Armstrong complained that his third wife, Alpha, thought more about "furs, diamonds and other flashy luxuries and not enough on me and my happiness. . . . She went through all my money and then walked out."[1] He divorced Alpha in the early 1940s and married Lucille Wilson on October 7, 1942.

Lucille was a good choice for a life mate. She loved and appreciated Armstrong the man. She knew that being a musical star was Armstrong's job. It was not the sum total of the man. Lucille immediately set out to take care of him. For decades he had not had a permanent home. She would find a sanctuary where he could relax and recover after months of traveling from job to job.

In 1943, when Armstrong returned from a tour, she instructed him to meet her at 3456 107th Street in the Corona neighborhood of Queens, in New York City. She promised to be waiting out front, but she was not there. He knocked on the door. Lucille opened the door and said, "Welcome home, honey."[2]

It was a real home. She had decorated it to be comfortable and had a hot, home-cooked meal waiting on the table. Armstrong looked it all over. He approved. He then invited the cab driver in to share the celebration dinner with them.

Corona was a mostly white neighborhood full of other musicians, both white and black. Among them were Count Basie, Tony Bennett, John Coltrane, Lena Horne, Billie Holiday, and Rudy Vallee.

Lucille spent the rest of her life making Armstrong comfortable. She knew that music and playing the

Lucille Armstrong created a refuge for her husband in a suburb of New York City. The house is now maintained by the Louis Armstrong House & Archives at Queens College.

trumpet came first with Armstrong. A wife with a good memory was useful on tours. She knew who all the big-wigs were. All Armstrong would have to do is ask her who this or that person was and she'd come up with the name and the person's importance to him and his career.

In 1945, the war was over. The time for large swing bands was also over. Glaser found it more and more difficult to get bookings for Armstrong and his large backing band. Clubs preferred the smaller "bebop" jazz groups. These modern jazzmen referred to Armstrong and the big bands as old "moldy figs."[3]

There was an increased interest in the beginnings of jazz. In 1947, a film called *New Orleans* was produced by the Hal Roach Studios, celebrating the origin of jazz. It was notable because it humanized and personalized its African-American characters. It featured Armstrong playing with a small group of musicians. However, the plot did not feature only African Americans in the cast. It starred Bing Crosby in a silly love story about a white crooner.

Promoter Leonard Feather suggested that Armstrong use a small band in concerts. Glaser and Armstrong weren't convinced it would work, but they agreed to experiment. On February 8, 1947, Armstrong per-formed at Carnegie Hall. For half the concert he used his big band. The other half featured Armstrong with a small group of musicians. The big-band grouping was panned by the critics while they praised the small one.

Armstrong and Glaser experimented with using a small band at a concert scheduled for May 7 at Town Hall in New York City. It sold out. A second concert was added on May 8, which also sold out. Because of these experiences, they decided to form a small band starring great jazz musicians.

On August 13, Louis Armstrong and his All Stars held their first concert in Billy Berg's Los Angeles Club. The group featured Armstrong's musical specialties. He did all the announcing. He led the group productions and sang with two other vocalists. With constant bookings, it became one of the hardest-working bands in jazz history.

Armstrong performed with Louis Armstrong's All Stars for the rest of his life. Among the original group was the trombonist Jack Teagarden. It was easy to convince Teagarden to disband his own big band, for keeping it had only put Teagarden deeper and deeper into debt. The two musicians had been friends for a long time, performing together off and on for years. Armstrong described their relationship: "He was from Texas, but it was always: 'You a spade and I'm an ofay. We got the same soul. Let's blow'—and that's the way it was."[4]

Barney Bigard was featured on clarinet. (He wrote his autobiography, called *With Louis and the Duke*, about

Louis Armstrong and his All Stars in the 1950s.

his adventures with the two jazz greats Armstrong and Ellington.) Big Sid Catlett supported the group with his special percussionist beat. Dick Cary doubled on piano and as a music arranger. Arvell Shaw, born in 1923 and the baby of the group, played the underlying bass violin. They imported a female singer, Velma Middleton, from a Los Angeles big band.

This small band rode the crest of the so-called Dixieland Revival of the New Orleans sound and continued to be popular for years. It was an integrated band, long before laws were passed to end segregation. In the jazz world, skin color did not matter. What mattered was how well you could play the music. Still, in some southern cities, gigs were canceled when it was discovered that blacks and whites performed in the same band.

Armstrong's international fame continued, too. In 1948 he returned to Europe to star in the Festival International du Jazz in Nice, France. His every number was cheered wildly.

Armstrong commissioned a young African American, Calvin Bailey, to create a large oil painting in 1948. It was a copy of a famous full-page photograph of Armstrong that had been published in the November 1935 issue of *Vanity Fair*. The picture showed Louis Armstrong holding his trumpet in one hand while the other mopped his cheek with his trademark handkerchief. The painting hung in his living room until his death.

In 1949, Armstrong was crowned king, twice. *Time* magazine featured Armstrong on its cover on February 21. The cover proclaimed him King of Jazz. The cover picture included a hand-drawn crown of trumpets nestled on his head. His portrait was sur-rounded by musical notes. Each note was beaming with a Louis Armstrong smile—except for the one blue note crying in the lower-left corner. The *Time* article discussed Armstrong's position as one of the founding fathers of Dixieland jazz. The nationwide publicity recharged his musical career. It also high-lighted other veteran jazz musicians, giving them a new lease on musical life. This was the first national mass-market magazine to honor him with a cover. It would not be the last.

He also was elected king of the Mardi Gras in his hometown of New Orleans. He had left New Orleans as a poor African American, traveling north to greener pastures. His first return to the city, in 1931, had been marred by racism and segregation. This time he returned as a hero. The mayor named him an honorary citizen of New Orleans and gave him the keys to the city.

He participated in every aspect of the Mardi Gras celebration that March. He attended parties before and after the parade. He greeted old friends and visited

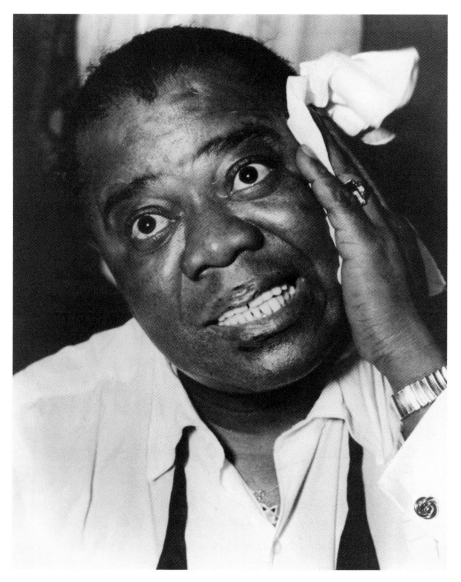

Louis Armstrong holds his trademark handkerchief. The scar on his lip came from too many years of using the pressure technique of horn playing.

old familiar places—those that had not been torn down with the refurbishing of New Orleans after the war.

When Armstrong was invited by the Zulu Aid Pleasure and Social Club to be the King of the Zulus, the press went wild. Photographs were flashed around the world. However, American civil rights leaders were offended. They had been working to end segregation and to bring dignity to all African Americans. They accused Armstrong of debasing himself for the amusement of southern whites.

Armstrong had been attacked before. Modern movies in the late 1940s were showing African Americans in serious roles. The new bebop style of jazz musicians did not smile and dance around the stage as Armstrong and the older jazz musicians had done. Bebop musicians presented themselves as angry young men. They played weird chords instead of catchy melodies. They objected to Armstrong's eager-to-please manner.

One of these angry young jazz men was Miles Davis. He spoke for all the bebop jazz musicians when he said:

> I hated the way they [the older jazz men] used to laugh and grin for audiences. I know *why* they did it—to make money and because they were entertainers as well as trumpet players. They had families to feed. Plus they . . . liked acting the clown. . . . I . . . didn't have to go through [the things] they had to go through to get

accepted in the music industry. They had already opened up a whole lot of doors for people like me to go through. . . . I didn't look at myself as an entertainer like they . . . did. [5]

All of his performing life, Armstrong had taken the stage with enthusiasm, wearing a huge grin that flashed constantly during his act. At almost fifty years old, he was still determined to entertain his audience, and he was not going to change his style.

7

AMBASSADOR
SATCHMO

By 1950, the big swing bands of Benny Goodman, Tommy Dorsey, Woody Herman, and Count Basie were out of business. Even Duke Ellington and his large orchestra fell upon hard times. Jazz and swing were not mainstream music anymore. Jitterbug and rock and roll were coming in. This was also music based on African-American styles, but it was sung by white men like Elvis Presley.

Armstrong stuck with his small All Stars group. Although his performing manner seemed out of sync with that of modern African-American performers, his music remained popular with jazz fans. The All Stars performed in nightclubs, concert halls, jazz festivals, and in a new venue—college campuses.

Armstrong was now a star, not just a musician. He played not only traditional jazz, but also his own versions of popular songs. He was working as hard as ever. Armstrong's fans were older people remembering the good old days. Younger fans discovered jazz when it was introduced to them in school, where Armstrong was introduced as the king of jazz. It is no wonder that everybody called him "Pops." In fact, he started it. He tended to call everyone Pops.

Armstrong was never very far from music. If he was not creating it himself onstage, he listened to it. Carrying a record player around on trips was not easy. Small, portable ones had not yet been invented. He had a special travel crate made for his player. When reel-to-reel tape recorders were invented, he added that to his special crate. He got into the habit of recording practice sessions and conversations.

Other changes influenced the music scene. Before World War II, one third of African Americans lived in the rural southern part of the United States. After the war, only one tenth lived there.[1] The rest had followed the job market up to the northern cities. These people had expected more freedom and opportunity in the cities. They often met the same frustrations that had fenced them in down south.

The migrants to the northern cities added their

Like most musicians on the road, Armstrong could not be separated from his music. Here in a special case are his reel-to-reel tape recorder and his record player—top-of-the-line equipment of the 1950s.

voices to those of the civil rights activists demanding the end of segregation and discrimination. They tried to force African-American movie and recording stars to join in the struggle. They became more vocal after the *Brown* v. *Board of Education of Topeka, Kansas* decision in 1954 by the Supreme Court of the United States. This decision ruled that separate accommodations, including schools for blacks and whites, were not equal. The Jim Crow laws were on their way to being eliminated.

Both Ellington and Armstrong were surprised at being accused of ignoring the struggle—even of being "Uncle Toms." (In the nineteenth-century novel *Uncle Tom's Cabin*, Uncle Tom keeps trying to appease the white slave owner and to persuade his fellow slaves to do the same. The term came to be used to describe black people who did not stand up for their rights but would allow themselves to be abused and pushed around by whites.)

Armstrong was proud of his success against the odds. He considered himself a groundbreaker in the civil rights struggle. He tried to set the record straight in an article he wrote for the major African-American magazine *Ebony*:

> Some folks . . . have even accused me of being an Uncle Tom. . . . How can they say that? I've pioneered in breaking the color line in many Southern states. . . . I've taken a lot of abuse, put up with a lot of jazz, even

been in some pretty dangerous spots through no fault of my own for almost forty years.[2]

Armstrong refused to limit himself to only African-American friends, as some African-American extremists advocated. He remained friends, without apology, with Bing Crosby and other white jazz fans.

He wrote constantly. His typewriter always traveled with him. In hotel rooms and backstage he typed magazine articles and his memoirs. He wrote long letters on customized "Satchmo" stationery.

His second autobiography was published in 1954—*Satchmo, My Life in New Orleans*. These colorful tales of his rags-to-riches story quickly became basic legends in any modern history of jazz. It was the most successful of any book on jazz at that time.

In September 1955, Armstrong recorded a song that became another popular hit. It was Kurt Weill's "Mack the Knife," from *The Threepenny Opera*. He told interviewers that his childhood experiences in New Orleans made it easy for him to capture Mack's unsavory essence.[3] People who read his autobiography understood instantly.

Armstrong's fans wanted him to play the song in concert, but the musical arrangements had been lost right after it was recorded. Fan pressure grew. Finally, in Miami, Armstrong figured out how to recover the sheet music. George Avakian of Columbia records remembered Armstrong's plan:

Louis and Lucille Armstrong board a plane for Stockholm, Sweden, in 1952. Armstrong and his band had not played in Germany since the 1930s. Because of Adolf Hitler and World War II, the band canceled its plans for a tour in the 1940s.

[Armstrong] goes to the cashier, gets two rolls of dimes, goes down to the coffee shop with the musicians and the sheet music and starts pouring dimes into the jukebox, and he tells the guys, "Copy out your part." The following night, he's finally able to play his smash hit.[4]

Another book, published in 1955, aroused more controversy than Armstrong's autobiography. Jeanette Eaton wrote a children's biography called *Trumpeter's Tale: The Story of Young Louis Armstrong*. It presented Armstrong as a positive role model for children. However, civil rights activists later complained that the illustrations were stereotypes of pickaninnies, an old word for African-American children that is now considered offensive. In fact, though, the illustrator had made his line drawings by working from Satchmo's own descriptions in his autobiography of his ragged, barefoot childhood.

In 1956, right before Armstrong's ancestral country, the colony of Gold Coast, became the republic of Ghana, he was invited to perform there. He was met at the airport by a huge crowd of people carrying signs that said welcome—*AKWABA!* Tribesmen picked him up and carried him by hand on a sedan chair.

More than one hundred thousand enthusiastic people attended the concert. This popularity in Africa helped counterbalance the bad reaction in the African-American community to his performance in the 1956 movie *High Society* with his old friend Bing Crosby.

Armstrong and his fellow musicians were a big hit in Africa
in 1956.

Armstrong opened the movie with a short prologue.
He kept appearing on screen giving commentary, sang
a duet with Crosby called "Now You Has Jazz," and
closed the story with a horn blast and the shout "End
of story!" It got rave reviews and was popular with
movie audiences. However, young African Americans
stayed away, offended by Armstrong's usual grin and
his clowning around. They wanted dramatic, forceful
movie stars like Sidney Poitier.

The review in the *Christian Science Monitor* praised
the movie for not treating the jazz band as if it were

In this publicity photo for the MGM movie *High Society*, Louis Armstrong shows his trumpet technique to actress Grace Kelly. Soon afterward, she became Princess Grace of Monaco.

pieces patched in, unrelated to the story line. Instead, it said, " . . . the Armstrong All-Stars are given the pre-ferred treatment they deserve in several full-length numbers, including a toe-tapping how-jazz-began sequence with Mr. Crosby."[5]

One of Armstrong's greatest fans was the singer Ella Fitzgerald. She and Armstrong made several records together during 1956 and 1957. Two other fans, Edward R. Murrow and Fred Friendly, who made feature-length film biographies, filmed a documentary on Armstrong in 1957. The result was called *Satchmo the Great*. It portrayed a man loved and respected throughout the world—a modest, thoughtful, gracious, and warm person.

The documentary mixed commentary with clips of Louis Armstrong on tour. The photography shows him looking tired and worn as he travels from concert to concert. Still, put him in front of an audience with a horn in his hand and his smile warms the whole place. The film showed the musician sharing his joy in music with the audience that is enjoying his performance.

The documentary emphasized Armstrong's posi-tion as one of the originators of jazz. It highlighted his identity as "Ambassador Satch" by following him on tour in Berlin and Africa. The film also showed him performing with the New York Philharmonic Orchestra. Jazz was now an honored part of musical tradition.

During his years of touring, Armstrong created collages of things that were important or had meaning to him. Some of them are in scrapbooks. Others are pasted on boxes. Band member Marty Napoleon thought he created them to help him remember events.[6] Armstrong himself explained, "My hobby is to pick out the different things during what I read and piece them together and make a little story of my own."[7]

One of them is a collage of newspaper clippings about Jackie Robinson's breaking the color barrier in major-league baseball. This tribute is displayed at Queens College in New York City along with about five hundred other collages. Armstrong's collages show that he was aware of every advance African Americans were making, even though he was careful not to associate himself with the more vocal civil rights activists.

In September 1957, he was scheduled to make a United States government–sponsored tour of the Soviet Union. However, earlier in the year while on tour, he saw a news story on television about the attempt to integrate schools in Little Rock, Arkansas.

Several African-American students had attempted to enroll at Central High School, an all-white school in Little Rock. They were prevented by a roaring mob and a line of police officers. The governor of the state, Orville Faubus, had declared that no African-American children would attend white schools in *his* state.

Armstrong was outraged.[8] He made his first public

Armstrong used his favorite mouthpiece to show Vice-President
Richard Nixon how to make the horn cry in 1957.

statements about race relations and civil rights. In
them he denounced Governor Faubus and the president of the United States, Dwight D. Eisenhower. He
added that he would cancel his scheduled tour to the
Soviet Union in protest.

Because he had never made a statement on this
subject before, it was quite effective. Many whites were
hostile to his statement, but African Americans
cheered.

8

HELLO, DOLLY!
GOOD-BYE, LOUIS

hroughout the 1950s and 1960s Louis Armstrong was a popular guest star on TV and in movies. He joked and clowned around with Ed Sullivan, Perry Como, Danny Kaye, and Flip Wilson.

With, and sometimes without, his All Stars, Armstrong continued the nonstop international schedule of concerts and recording sessions. They toured Africa. Concerts were held in Nigeria, Central Africa, Ghana, and Kenya. Each time they were greeted enthusiastically. It was as if a talented and successful son had returned home.

This was even apparent in highly segregated

Southern Rhodesia, a British colony, which is now called Zimbabwe. In 1960 the United States Embassy received word that Louis Armstrong and his All Stars would come to Southern Rhodesia, provided the audience included both black and white Africans. This created a dilemma. Would the British government allow it? Would an audience show up? Would there be security problems?

The British government gave permission, and the embassy scheduled three concerts. When Armstrong arrived and was informed of the decision, he said, "It's a good thing you won, or I wouldn't be here!"[1]

At the opening concert in the capital city of Salisbury, the standard ropes separating blacks and whites were gone. Twenty-five thousand people filled the soccer stadium—blacks interspersed with whites. It was the first truly integrated gathering in the country.

Armstrong sang his hits "Mack the Knife" and "Blueberry Hill." The audience sang along. The ninety-minute concert continued with encore after encore. Finally, Armstrong's husky voice whispered through the loudspeakers, "I gotta tell y'all something. . . . It's sure nice to see this."[2] The crowd roared in agreement.

Meanwhile, the personnel of the All Stars continued to change over the years. Doing practically the same program every night became boring for some. Others just did not feel they could keep up with the constant touring.

Louis Armstrong helped spread jazz music throughout the world.

Armstrong may have been one of the most constantly photographed people on earth. This was mainly because he always kept the audience in mind. He made himself available to both amateur and professional photographers, always willing to participate in the public relations side of show business. Many fans sent him copies of pictures taken of themselves with him. He saved these copies. They are now in the Louis Armstrong Archives in Queens College in New York City.

Armstrong's optimistic spirit kept him clowning around both on stage and off. In effect, he was always "on," thriving on attention. The show business glamour and his trademark smile were rooted in his own friendly personality. He always seemed to be at ease with people.

In the early 1960s he and Duke Ellington got together for a quick session and made a record. In 1962 he was invited to Disneyland in California. He reunited with Johnny St. Cyr and Kid Ory for a Dixieland concert on Disney's recreated riverboat, the *Mark Twain*.

In 1963 he recorded the popular song "Hello, Dolly!" It became a smash hit in 1964. For a time it knocked the Beatles' "She Loves You" out of first place on the *Billboard* Top 40.

The Society of African Culture held its first World Festival of Negro Arts in Senegal during April 1966. It

Armstrong's music appealed to the young and the old. Here he autographs the head of a fan with a mohawk hairstyle in 1961.

honored the achievements of Louis Armstrong, but he was not able to attend. Ellington and his orchestra performed instead.

The April 15, 1966, issue of *Life* magazine featured a special full-length foldout cover of Armstrong. The unusual angle of the photograph, taken from above, was such that the cover showed him playing his horn, from the shoulders up. The folded out section showed the rest of him.

In 1968, Armstrong's recording of "What a Wonderful World" became an international hit.

However, by this time health problems were beginning to show. During a summer tour of England he looked frail. In September, he collapsed with a heart attack. Even after he was released from the hospital, his doctor insisted that Armstrong take at least half a year off, stop eating salt, and lose weight. His kidneys were also failing. His body had swelled up with fluid. He was in and out of hospitals.

When Armstrong was asked to record the theme song for a James Bond film in 1969, his doctor would not allow him to play. Instead he sang "We Have All the Time in the World." By this time his voice had become as gritty as sandpaper.

Unfortunately, Armstrong did *not* have all the time in the world. His time on earth was drawing to a close. He knew his own health was failing. One of the stresses that added to it was the death of Joe Glaser, his friend, advisor, and manager.

Louis Armstrong had trusted Glaser to keep things in order and honest while he performed music. He discovered that his white manager was worthy of that trust. At Glaser's death, all the monies and papers he had been controlling were turned over to the Armstrong family. Glaser had not made himself rich at Armstrong's expense. He had paid all the expenses of the tours and had taken as income his 15 percent management fee. All the rest had been put in trust for the Armstrongs.

Armstrong used $40,000 of this money to establish the Louis Armstrong Educational Foundation. This foundation is administered by Queens College in New York City.

Armstrong's last movie was *Hello, Dolly!* in 1969. In the film, Barbra Streisand enters the ballroom singing the title song. To one side is an orchestra accompanying her. When the orchestra leader turns around, the audience discovers it is Satchmo—handsomely attired in a black tuxedo with red cummerbund and a red carnation. The trademark smile is there as the two sing a duet. After almost fifty years in films, he was still giving it his very best shot.

America was taking note of its living treasure. Armstrong was honored at the 1970 Newport Jazz Festival. Thin but energetic, he sang at the "Salute to Satch" night. There was a tribute from modern trumpet players in *Down Beat* magazine. The July 4, 1970, issue of *Saturday Review* magazine had a cover story on his seventieth birthday. (To the end he insisted he was born on July 4, 1900.)

A reporter once asked what he thought was the secret of his success. Armstrong replied, "I didn't wish for anything I couldn't get, and I got pretty near everything I wanted because I worked for it."[3]

Even though his health was getting worse, he continued to sing and occasionally play his trumpet. In the fall of 1970 he recorded an introduction on a

Louis and Lucille Armstrong share a quiet moment at home in 1970. On the wall behind them hangs the portrait of Armstrong painted by African-American artist Calvin Bailey in 1948.

reissue of his hit "What a Wonderful World." It preserved his optimistic philosophy for all time:

> Seems to me it ain't the world that's so bad, but what we are doing to it. And all I'm saying is, see what a wonderful world it would be if only we would give it a chance. Love, baby, love. That's the secret. Yeah.[4]

He continued to book dates for his All Stars. Against his doctor's advice, he continued to play his trumpet. The last gig was two weeks in March 1971 at the Waldorf-Astoria's Empire Room in New York City. His doctor, Gary Zucker, warned him that he could drop dead in the middle of performing.

Armstrong replied, "Doc, you don't understand. My whole life, my whole soul, my whole spirit is to blow that horn. I've got to do it."[5]

On March 15, Armstrong entered Beth Israel Hospital in New York City. His heart was failing. He was suffering from liver and kidney disease. It was two months before he recovered enough from these ailments and the lung infection that accompanied them to be allowed to go home.

While Armstrong was hospitalized, he missed the New Orleans Jazz and Heritage Festival, which had been planned as a tribute to his life and music. Kid Ory filled in for him. It was Ory's first visit back home in fifty-two years.

Armstrong spent the next several months enjoying Lucille's red beans and rice. He walked around the neighborhood or sat on the stoop of his home in Corona talking to the neighborhood children.

Several television newscasters interviewed him on his July 4, 1971, birthday. A frail but smiling Armstrong told the world he planned to entertain them again soon. Two days later, at 5:30 in the morning, July 6, he died peacefully in his sleep.

President Richard Nixon declared that Armstrong

A trumpeter uses Louis Armstrong's old cornet to play taps during the memorial service for Armstrong held in New Orleans.

Louis Armstrong arrives in heaven and out-trumpets the
Archangel Gabriel. Cartoonist Paul Conrad created this editorial
cartoon in 1971 after Armstrong's death. It was reprinted in
many newspapers.

was "one of the architects of an American art form, a free and individual spirit, and an artist of worldwide fame."[6] He made arrangements for Armstrong's body to lie in state at the New York City National Guard Armory at Sixty-sixth Street and Park Avenue. More than twenty-five thousand people filed by to pay their respects on July 8.

Political leaders, entertainers, and fans from around the world sent messages of condolence to Armstrong's widow, Lucille. Coretta Scott King sent a letter that said, in part, "[The] eloquence of his horn [helped] bridge generation, racial, political, and national gaps."[7]

Armstrong had envisioned a good, old-fashioned New Orleans jazz funeral for himself, complete with a parade to and from the cemetery. In fact, he was buried in Flushing Cemetery with very little music. New Orleans, however, held a huge parade the next Sunday. Many of the old jazzmen marched and blew that day for this son of New Orleans who brought jazz to the world.

A cartoon in the *Los Angeles Times* personified the world's reaction to its loss. The artist, Paul Conrad, had drawn Armstrong in heaven out-trumpeting the angel Gabriel. The world's loss was heaven's gain.

9

ARMSTRONG'S
IMPACT ON
AMERICAN MUSIC

he Louis Armstrong story does not end with his death in 1971. Within that same year the Louis Armstrong Middle School was established in Queens, New York. It is run with the assistance of Queens College staff and is a magnet school for New York City teens. Every morning before classes the children sing Armstrong's famous song "What a Wonderful World."

On July 4, 1976, as part of the United States bicentennial celebration, New Orleans dedicated a statue to Louis Armstrong. This statue of Armstrong standing, holding a horn and his trademark handkerchief, was the first public work of the African-American sculptor

Elizabeth Catlett. It was begun in 1970 and financed by Bing Crosby and other Hollywood entertainers. It is located in the Back o' Town area of New Orleans. A thirty-one-acre park was created around it in 1980.

By the end of Armstrong's life, he was making good money. He could have lived anywhere. Still, even though the neighborhood deteriorated, he stayed in the Corona area of Queens. Lucille had made this three-story house a home for him. She stayed in their home until she died in 1983.

After that, the house and all its contents were donated to Queens College. The house is now the Louis Armstrong Historic House Museum run by Queens College and the New York City Department of Cultural Affairs. It will open to the public in the year 2000. Remembering that Louis Armstrong loved children, the college holds jazz concerts for young people in the garden of the museum.[1]

It took quite a few years to organize all the Louis Armstrong material donated to Queens College. Armstrong had been collecting for decades. There were 85 scrapbooks, 650 reel-to-reel audio tapes, 1,600 records (78s, LPs, and 45s), more than 5,000 photographs, 5 trumpets, and 120 awards and plaques. In addition there were 400 books, journals, and personal papers.

The Louis Armstrong collection is stored in the Archival Center in the Benjamin S. Rosenthal Library

In tribute to the king of jazz, these murals were painted on the walls of the Louis Armstrong Middle School in Queens, New York.

at Queens College. This collection was opened to scholars and researchers in 1994. Part of the collection was exhibited in Queens in 1994. Then it became a Smithsonian Institution Traveling Exhibition from 1994 to 1996. The exhibition included almost four hundred photographs, letters, memorabilia, trumpets, audio broadcasts, recordings, paintings, and sculptures from the archives for the display.

The archives do not just illustrate Armstrong's triumphs. They record his daily battles and the prejudices that an African-American musician had to fight in order to pursue his craft. Shirley Strum Kenny, president of Queens College, when talking about his entries in his diaries and journals, said, "Louis's rough-edged voice filled with wit, comedy, insight, and affection, comes through as clearly in his writings as in his music."[2] Armstrong loved to write.[3] Music was his work, but he wrote to relax. He could toss off a thirteen-page single-spaced letter or a short note written in green ink.

Although Louis Armstrong had died, the sound of his trumpet and his voice lived on. In 1989, his song "What a Wonderful World" was featured in the movie *Good Morning, Vietnam*. The song was quickly reissued and stayed on *Billboard*'s Top 100 for more than six weeks.

In September 1995, a Louis Armstrong commemorative stamp was issued. On the first day a newly issued

This statue is mounted on a wall of the Louis Armstrong Middle School in Queens, New York.

stamp can be used, a special design is used to cancel it at the post office. Often this design extends well into the body of the envelope.

The design of the Louis Armstrong First Day cancel was created by a local sixth grader, Rafael Hernandez. He was invited to attend the opening-day ceremonies at the Louis Armstrong house. Postmaster William Rogers ended his speech with these words: "Let us dedicate this stamp honoring the legendary Ambassador of American Music, Louis Armstrong."[4]

It is acknowledged that jazz is the only truly American music. Louis Armstrong is the embodiment of its development. He was in New Orleans when the hot new music was invented. He became part of the Chicago jazz movement. He helped spread jazz music throughout the United States through tours and radio broadcasts.

His improvisational flights moved jazz from group to solo playing. Even though he went on to embrace swing and had successful pop songs, his technique influenced jazzmen, pop and rock singers, and music arrangers for years. His joy in performing and his unabashed love of life moved him from being a simple musician to a star entertainer.

Music critic Richard Merryman once stated that most of the music that is played today comes from something Louis Armstrong created. Dan Morgenstern declared that "there is not a single musician playing in the jazz tradition who does not make daily use, knowingly or unknowingly, of something invented by Louis Armstrong."[5]

Dizzy Gillespie said it best. When asked to place Louis Armstrong in history, Gillespie declared: "No him, no me."[6]

CHRONOLOGY

1901—Louis Armstrong is born on August 4.

1903—Beatrice Armstrong, Louis's sister, is born.

1913—Sent to the Colored Waifs' Home for Boys.

1914—Begins professional career as cornet player.

1916—Meets Joe Oliver.

1918—Marries Daisy Parker; replaces Oliver in Kid Ory's Band.

1919—Joins Fate Marable's dance orchestra on a Mississippi riverboat.

1922—Joins Oliver's Creole Jazz Band in Chicago.

1923—Tours with Oliver's band, and they make their first recordings.

1924—Marries Lillian Hardin; joins the Fletcher Henderson Orchestra in New York City.

1925—Returns to Chicago; makes first Hot Five recordings; first plays a trumpet.

1927—Armstrong's mother, Mayann, dies in Chicago.

1928—Records "West End Blues."

1929—Stars in *Hot Chocolates* on Broadway in New York City; switches to big-band format.

1931—Returns to New Orleans to perform.

1932—Begins first European tour.

1933—Begins second European tour.

1935—Signs management contract with Joe Glaser.

1936—First autobiography published: *Swing That Music*.

1938—Marries Alpha Smith, but the marriage last only a few years.

1942—Marries Lucille Wilson.

1943—Moves to Corona, Queens, New York City.

1947—Debut of Louis Armstrong and his All Stars.

1949—A *Time* magazine cover crowns him King of Jazz, February 21.

1954—Second autobiography published: *Satchmo, My Life in New Orleans*.

1960—Tours Africa, performing first integrated concert in the segregated British colony of Rhodesia.

1964—"Hello, Dolly!" becomes a number-one song.

1968—"What a Wonderful World" becomes a hit worldwide.

1971—Louis Armstrong dies on July 6.

Louis Armstrong Performs

Selected Discography

All-Time Best of Louis Armstrong (Curb/Warner Bros., 1990)

The California Concerts (GRP, 1992)

The Complete Decca Studio Recordings of Louis Armstrong and the All-Stars (6-CD set)

The Complete RCA Victor Recordings (RCA, 1997)

The Essential Louis Armstrong (Vanguard, 1987)

Highlights from His Decca Years (MCA/GRP, 1994)

Let's Do It: Best of the Verve Years (Verve, 1995)

Louis Armstrong & King Oliver (Milestone, 1992)

Louis Armstrong, Greatest Hits (RCA, 1996)

Louis Armstrong of New Orleans (MCA, 1990)

Portrait of the Artist as a Young Man, 1923–1934 (Columbia/Legacy, 1994)

Satch Plays Fats (Columbia/Legacy, 1987)

Satchmo at Symphony Hall (Decca Jazz, 1996)

Satchmo the Great (Columbia Legacy, 1994)

This Is Jazz 1—Louis Armstrong (Columbia/Legacy, 1996)

20 Golden Pieces of Louis Armstrong (Bulldog, 1996)

The 25 Greatest Hot Fives & Hot Sevens (ASV Living Era, 1995)

What a Wonderful World (MCA, 1994)

The Wonderful Louis Armstrong (Blue Moon, 1994)

Selected Filmography

High Society (MGM, 1956)

Five Pennies (Paramount, 1959)

Hello, Dolly! (Fox Video, 1969)

Trumpet Kings (RCA/Ariola International, 1985)

CHAPTER NOTES

Chapter 1. A Horn in the Night
1. Hugues Panassie, *Louis Armstrong* (New York: Charles Scribner's Sons, 1971), p. 9.

2. Max Jones and John Chilton, *Louis: The Louis Armstrong Story 1900–1971* (London: November Books, 1971), p. 58.

3. Sam Tanenhaus, *Louis Armstrong, Musician* (New York: Chelsea House, 1989), p. 57.

Chapter 2. On the Streets of New Orleans
1. Louis Armstrong, *Satchmo: My Life in New Orleans* (New York: Prentice Hall, 1954), p. 38.

2. Gary Giddins, *Satchmo* (New York: Doubleday, 1988), pp. 47–53.

3. Laurence Bergreen, *Louis Armstrong: An Extravagant Life* (New York: Broadway Books, 1997), p. 15.

4. Armstrong, p. vii.

5. Robert Hoskins, *Louis Armstrong, Biography of a Musician* (Los Angeles: Halloway House Publishing, 1979), p. 32.

6. Armstrong, p. 15.

7. Bergreen, p. 16.

8. Max Jones and John Chilton, *Louis: The Louis Armstrong Story 1900–1971* (London: November Books, 1971), p. 43.

9. Giddins, p. 63.

Chapter 3. His Choice Was Music
1. Laurence Bergreen, *Louis Armstrong: An Extravagant Life* (New York: Broadway Books, 1997), p. 73.

2. Max Jones and John Chilton, *Louis: The Louis Armstrong Story 1900–1971* (London: November Books, 1971), p. 15.

3. Louis Armstrong, *Swing That Music* (New York: Da Capo Press, 1993), p. 31.

4. Sam Tanenhaus, *Louis Armstrong, Musician* (New York: Chelsea House, 1989), p. 45.

5. Louis Armstrong, *Satchmo: My Life in New Orleans* (New York: Prentice-Hall, 1954), p. 100.

6. Armstrong, *Swing That Music*, p. 34.

7. Dan Morgenstern, "Yesterday, Today, and Tomorrow," *Down Beat*, July 15, 1965, p. 18.

8. Armstrong, *Satchmo*, pp. x–xi.

Chapter 4. Jazz in the Roaring Twenties

1. Louis Armstrong, *Satchmo: My Life in New Orleans* (New York: Prentice-Hall, 1954), pp. 236-237.

2. Robert Hoskins, *Louis Armstrong, Biography of a Musician* (Los Angeles: Holloway House Publishing, 1979), p. 121.

3. Louis Armstrong, *Swing That Music* (New York: Da Capo Press, 1993), p. 8.

4. Max Jones and John Chilton, *Louis: The Louis Armstrong Story 1900–1971* (London: November Books, 1971), p. 81.

5. Hoskins, p. 133.

6. Armstrong, *Swing That Music*, pp. 84–85.

7. Caroline Scannell, "Armstrong First Day Ceremony in Queens, New York," *Stamps*, September 30, 1995, p. 14.

8. Rudy Vallee, introduction to Louis Armstrong, *Swing That Music*, p. xvi.

9. Hoskins, p. 121.

Chapter 5. Big Bands

1. Richard Merryman, *Louis Armstrong: A Self-Portrait* (New York: Eakins Press, 1971), p. 40.

2. Ibid., p. 41.

3. Rex Stewart, "Boy Meets King," *Down Beat*, July 15,1965, p. 23.

4. Marc H. Miller, "Louis Armstrong: A Portrait Record," *Louis Armstrong: A Cultural Legacy* (New York: Queens Museum of Art, 1994), p. 188.

5. Donald Bogle, "Louis Armstrong: The Films," *Louis Armstrong: A Cultural Legacy* (New York: Queens Museum of Art, 1994), p.152.

6. Max Jones and John Chilton, *Louis: The Louis Armstrong Story 1900–1971* (London: November Books, 1971), p. 119.

7. Merryman, p. 32.

8. Jones and Chilton, p. 136.

9. "Louis Armstrong: 'My Chops Was Beat—But I'm Dyin' to Swing Again' " (The Classic Interviews—*Down Beat* 60th Anniversary Issue), *Down Beat*, February 1994, p. 22.

10. Louis Armstrong, *Satchmo: My Life in New Orleans* (New York: Da Capo Press, 1986), p. xi.

Chapter 6. King of Jazz

1. Laurence Bergreen, *Louis Armstrong: An Extravagant Life* (New York: Broadway Books, 1997), p. 392.

2. Caroline Scannell, "Armstrong First Day Ceremony in Queens, New York," *Stamps*, September 30, 1995, p. 14.

3. Dan Morgenstern, "Louis Armstrong and the Development and Diffusion of Jazz," *Louis Armstrong, a Cultural Legacy* (New York: Queens Museum of Art, 1994), p. 133.

4. Max Jones and John Chilton, *Louis: The Louis Armstrong Story 1900–1971* (New York: Da Capo Press, 1971, 1988). p. 58.

5. Miles Davis and Quincy Troupe, *Miles: The Autobiography* (New York: Simon & Schuster, 1989), p. 83.

Chapter 7. Ambassador Satchmo

1. Richard Long, "Louis Armstrong and African-American Culture," *Louis Armstrong: A Cultural Legacy* (New York: Queens Museum of Art, 1994), p. 83.

2. Louis Armstrong, "Daddy, How the Country Has Changed!" *Ebony*, May 1961, p. 85.

3. Dan Morgenstern, "Louis Armstrong and the Development and Diffusion of Jazz," *Louis Armstrong: A Cultural Legacy* (New York: Queens Museum of Art, 1994), p. 142.

4. Laurence Bergreen, *Louis Armstrong: An Extravagant Life* (New York: Broadway Books, 1997), p. 459.

5. Donald Bogle, "Louis Armstrong: The Films," *Louis Armstrong: A Cultural Legacy* (New York: Queens Museum of Art, 1994), p. 174.

6. Marc H. Miller, "Louis Armstrong: A Portrait Record," *Louis Armstrong: A Cultural Legacy* (New York: Queens Museum of Art, 1994), p. 209.

7. Letter from Armstrong to Mrs. Marili Mardon, c/o Jazzman Record Shop, September 27, 1953 (in the Louis Armstrong Archives, Queens College, City University of New York).

8. Gary Giddins, *Satchmo* (New York: Doubleday, 1988), pp. 160, 163.

Chapter 8. Hello, Dolly! Good-bye, Louis

1. Mark B. Lewis, "The Concert: Louis Armstrong in Rhodesia," *American Heritage*, May–June 1996, p. 38.

2. Ibid.

3. Terry Teachout, "Top Brass," *The New York Times Book Review*, August 3, 1997, p. 4.

4. Marc H. Miller, "Louis Armstrong: A Cultural Legacy," *Louis Armstrong: A Cultural Legacy* (New York: Queens Museum of Art, 1994), p. 63.

5. Laurence Bergreen, *Louis Armstrong: An Extravagant Life* (New York: Broadway Books, 1997), p. 492.

6. Sam Tanenhaus, *Louis Armstrong, Musician* (New York, Chelsea House, 1989), p. 122.

7. Letter from Coretta Scott King to Lucille Armstrong, July 8, 1971 (in the Louis Armstrong Archives, Queens College, City University of New York).

Chapter 9. Armstrong's Impact on American Music

1. Shirley Strum Kenny, forward to *Louis Armstrong: A Cultural Legacy* (New York: Queens Museum of Art, 1994), p. 12.

2. Ibid., p. 13.

3. Dan Morgenstern, introduction to Armstrong, *Satchmo: My Life in New Orleans* (New York: Da Capo Press, 1986), p. x.

4. Caroline Scannell, "Armstrong First Day Ceremony in Queens, New York," *Stamps*, September 30, 1995, p. 14.

5. Dan Morgenstern, "Louis Armstrong and the Development and Diffusion of Jazz," *Louis Armstrong: A Cultural Legacy* (New York: Queens Museum of Art, 1994), p. 95.

6. Jeff Levenson, "Jazz Blue Notes," *Billboard*, October 8, 1994, p. 58.

Further Reading

Armstrong, Louis. *Satchmo: My Life in New Orleans.* New York: Da Capo Press, 1986 (new edition of 1954 autobiography).

———. *Swing That Music.* New York: Da Capo Press, 1993 (new edition of 1936 autobiography).

Bergreen, Laurence. *Louis Armstrong: An Extravagant Life.* New York: Broadway Books, 1997.

Brown, Sandford. *Louis Armstrong: Swinging Singing Satchmo.* New York: Franklin Watts, 1993.

Feather, Leonard. *From Satchmo to Miles.* New York: Stine and Day, 1972.

Giddins, Gary. *Satchmo.* New York: Doubleday, 1988.

Jones, Max, and John Chilton. *Louis, The Louis Armstrong Story 1900–1971.* New York: Da Capo Press, 1988 (reprint of 1971 biography).

McKissack, Patricia, and Fredrick McKissack. *Louis Armstrong, Jazz Musician.* Springfield, N.J.: Enslow Publishers, 1991.

Miller, Marc H., ed. *Louis Armstrong: A Cultural Legacy.* New York: Queens Museum of Art, 1994.

Tanenhaus, Sam. *Louis Armstrong, Musician.* New York: Chelsea House, 1989.

Terkel, Studs. *Giants of Jazz*. New York: HarperCollins, 1975.

Video

Marsalis on Music: Sousa to Satchmo (Sony, 1995).

On the Internet

<http://www.qc.edu/Library/info/liblaarc.html>

Satchmo's site at Queens College. This is where you can look, listen, and learn about the treasure trove of materials found in his home in Corona, Queens.

INDEX